AF541780

STATE OF THE CAPITAL

Praise for the Book

This book is an enchanting portrayal of a monolith organization administered in modern days by people with myopic vision lacking commitment. In this accurate depiction of the reasons for the malaise plaguing the historic civic body, the author has correctly diagnosed the underlying factors for the malady. He has also made concrete and practical suggestions to make it more responsive to the citizens and common man. It is a delight to go through the absorbing work of the author, who brought about a transformation in the dilapidated administration of the capital city using his skills and experience with aplomb.

—Dr Harsh Vardhan,
Minister of Health and Family Welfare,
Government of India

K.S. Mehra, who was Commissioner of the unified Municipal Corporation of Delhi (MCD) during 2008–12, held the post with great distinction. This book is a testimony to his commitment in dealing with complex issues and challenges he faced during his tenure. His deft handling of the situation is a lesson for all urban planners. A must-read!

—Kapil Sibal,
Member of Parliament, and
former Union Cabinet Minister for Science & Technology
and Earth Sciences, Human Resource Development,
Telecom & IT and Law & Justice

STATE OF THE CAPITAL

Creating a Truly Smart City

K.S. MEHRA

~Foreword by RAJNATH SINGH~

RUPA

Published by
Rupa Publications India Pvt. Ltd 2019
7/16, Ansari Road, Daryaganj
New Delhi 110002

Sales Centres:
Allahabad Bengaluru Chennai
Hyderabad Jaipur Kathmandu
Kolkata Mumbai

Photo courtesy: Library, North Delhi Municipal Corporation

ISBN: 978-93-5333-627-1

First impression 2019

10 9 8 7 6 5 4 3 2 1

Printed at Parksons Graphics Pvt. Ltd., Mumbai

This book is dedicated to the sweet memories of my mother Khazano Devi, who could not see me grow and stand on my feet, and to my wife Renu, who nudged me all through the work to reflect on issues that could make the city a better place to live in.

CONTENTS

FOREWORD

Given the present state of municipal services in our towns and cities, the need for bringing in qualitative improvement can hardly be overemphasized. Efficient, responsive and effective delivery of civic services to citizens requires far-reaching systematic changes in our municipal policy framework.

Written by a senior retired bureaucrat with first-hand knowledge and experience of municipal affairs, *State of the Capital* painstakingly describes the areas considered important for laying a strong foundation for bringing about systematic improvements in the strategies necessary for a responsive system to provide a healthy living environment in our cities.

I am confident that the suggestions and solutions provided by the author would prove to be useful to the policymakers, local self-government officials, etc. in the country, rooted as they are in the ground with the practical realities of day-to-day life. I am also hopeful that the book will encourage discussion and debate on the direction that the policymakers must adopt in the years ahead, to provide the right kind of solutions to the problems besetting the cities.

With good wishes...

Rajnath Singh
Defence Minister of India

INTRODUCTION: THE HARD TRUTHS

My tenure in the Municipal Corporation of Delhi (MCD) can be best described as the most fulfilling and satisfying, from a professional point of view. However, the idea to write this book germinated when I was asked to deliver a lecture on Urban Governance before a select audience at the India International Centre (IIC) on 15 May 2015. While preparing for the lecture, I realized that the depth of experience and insights I gained from working as the commissioner of the unified MCD for over four years (2008–12) must be shared and preserved for posterity. To a layperson, urban governance would simply mean the availability and efficient delivery of utilities and services. This is a tall order. The governance of the capital city is a formidable task, full of challenges. The urban scenario, with its ever-changing situations and requirements, presents a canvas which is difficult to comprehend, and so keeping pace with it requires regular updation of resources, inventories and also strategies.

AN URBAN CHAOS WAITING TO SELF-DESTRUCT

The city of Delhi has an area of 1,484 sq. km. The entire area of Delhi, excluding the areas under the jurisdiction of the New Delhi Municipal Council (NDMC) (3 per cent) and the Delhi Cantonment Board (DCB) (3 per cent), comes under the jurisdiction of the MCD (now trifurcated); which means 94 per cent of the total area of the city is under the jurisdiction of the MCD. As per the Master Plan of Delhi/ MPD 2021, the total available urbanizable area by 2021 will be 9,779 sq. km; i.e., 65.94 per cent of the total area of the city.

As per the report of the Tejendra Khanna Committee of experts set up by the Government of India to look into various aspects of unauthorized constructions and Misuse of Premises in Delhi (dated 13 May 2006), as against 438 regular and approved colonies on 1 January 1994 there were as many as 1,641 unauthorized colonies awaiting regularization. There were also sixty resettlement colonies and around 1,200 jhuggi jhopries (JJ clusters). It is estimated that more area than is available for urbanization has already been urbanized. The growth in the city's population over the years has also been extraordinary, primarily due to migration, which continues since the Partition of India. As per the 2011 census, there were 168 lakh persons living in the city, with just 4.19 lakh persons living in rural areas around the city. The density of population in these areas is 11,297 persons per sq. km, which increases to 17,664 persons per sq. km in the urban areas.[1] But the city has not always been a concrete jungle.

The capital city was meticulously planned with due emphasis on the rigid segregation of residential, commercial and public areas. In the Master Plan approved in 1962, the objective was not to develop the city colony by colony, but rather zone by zone, making each zone self-sufficient; i.e., each zone would have its own social, educational and health infrastructure. Additionally, each zone had its own Zonal Development Plan. There is undoubtedly a need for flexibility in the rules for some deserving cases with valid reasons. The problem, however, arises when defiance of the rules becomes the rule. The cumulative ill effect of such misdemeanours is beyond imagination, as is evident in the case of the country's capital. Within a decade of the Master Plan 1962, it was estimated that 25 per cent of the city's land and around 45 per cent of the buildings were not in accordance with the plan.

The situation has worsened over the years with more than 75 per cent of the city being taken over by unplanned growth. Sadly, the provisions of successive Master Plans

---

[1]As per census 2011: Delhi Human Development Report 2013, Page 124

have been routinely flouted, presenting an apocalyptic picture of Delhi as an urban chaos waiting to self-destruct.

Every monsoon, the municipalities and the government spend huge sums to protect lives and property on the Yamuna flood plains from the fury of floods. This money literally goes down the drain, as there is absolutely no permanent solution to ward off floods in such areas other than to shift the course of the river itself. It is a sad commentary on the system that permitted the establishment of such settlements in the first place, which have had an adverse impact on the ecology besides draining public funds. The unplanned settlements impact the efficiency of services such as sanitation and sewerage, maintenance and water supply. They also hinder access to habitation during emergencies that require outside assistance from various agencies, such as the fire brigade and ambulance services.

No efforts have been made to initiate reconstruction of unsafe and structurally unfit buildings in the earthquake-prone regions of Delhi-NCR (National Capital Region). There is an urgent need to check buildings and infrastructure for safety against a high-intensity earthquake, and also for structurally unsafe constructions to be either retrofitted or reconstructed. Occupants of such settlements should not be patronized by any pressure group. This urgent course correction needs to be initiated by building a strong public opinion in its favour.

Although the preparation of the Local Area Plan (LAP)

for thirty-three wards was a step in the right direction by the erstwhile unified MCD, it got mired in issues related to jurisdiction. This initiative had aimed to demonstrate a model based upon which all the unplanned areas of the city would be rebuilt or retrofitted in conformity with the prescriptions of the National Building Code of India (NBC)[2] 2005, the Vulnerability Atlas of India[3] 2006 and the building bye-laws.

There is a shortage of dwelling units in the capital. According to the 2011 Census estimates, the number of houses available at a particular time was lesser than the households in need of accommodation. For instance, 3,341 million households resided in 3,176 million houses.[4] This meant that migrants encroached upon all forms of land available within city spaces. The growth of slums has progressed unabated, despite continuous efforts of successive governments to make Delhi a slum-free state. This also puts pressure on civic amenities and causes wasteful expenditure.

Roads in the city require extensive repairs after every monsoon season, leading to colossal recurring waste of

---

[2]The National Building Code (NBC) comprises a set of regulations to be adopted by various departments, municipal administration and public bodies. It lays down minimum provisions to protect public safety with regard to structural sufficiency of buildings.

[3]The Vulnerability Atlas of India is a collation of hazard scenario for the whole country and presents the digitized state- or union territory-wise hazard maps with respect to natural calamities, such as earthquakes, heavy winds and floods.

[4]Delhi Human Development Report 2013, p. 124, para 5.2.1

precious public revenues, which could have been better utilized for providing education and healthcare facilities. The almost non-functional, archaic drainage system results in waterlogging, which in turn damages city roads, besides creating a breeding ground for mosquitoes that cause malaria and dengue. The peripheral nallahs (streams/drains) meant for receiving both storm water and waste water move at the level of roads. The poor condition of the roads also causes noise and air pollution, affecting the health of residents.

With each passing year, the number of vehicles in the city registers an exponential growth, with almost no parking spaces available anywhere. The encroachments on the roads further narrow down the right of way, leading to incidents of road rage. The air and noise pollution generated by around 80,000 trucks[5] entering the city every day makes it necessary to provide bypasses around Delhi to ensure that vehicles not bound for Delhi do not enter the city. The recently completed Eastern and Western Peripheral Expressways should hopefully divert such traffic. The share of public transport has decreased substantially, leading to increased emissions and road fatalities from private transport.

Garbage dumping and open defecation are other causes of pollution. The pathetic sights along the railway tracks

[5]TNN, 'Carriers of toxic air, trucks can't enter Delhi for 3 days after Diwali', *The Times of India*, 6 November 2018, accessed in June 2019, https://timesofindia.indiatimes.com/city/delhi/carriers-of-toxic-air-trucks-cant-enter-delhi-for-3-days-after-diwali/articleshow/66529571.cms

force tourists to believe that there is no system of waste management in the city. We desperately need innovative solutions to tackle this problem. For instance, all the railway tracks from Delhi up to a distance of 5 km can be entrenched in walls on both sides and the space thus created can be leased out annually for commercial advertisements, thereby generating revenue for the maintenance of the tracks. A win-win situation!

BRINGING METHOD TO THE MADNESS

The efforts of the government need to be well placed right from the planning stage itself to ensure the right kind of investment in the prioritized sectors. For example, there is no need to further augment road infrastructure in the city, which is adequate enough to cater to the requirements for many years to come. There is, however, a need to invest more in public transport—buses, metro, monorail, etc.—to ensure last-mile connectivity. The charges of parking facilities should be commensurate with the level of congestion in the area and the duration of parking. So, the cost of parking a car in South Delhi should be higher than any other location in the city.

Proliferation of industrial activities causing pollution and negatively impacting the environment in the city has been a subject of extensive debate. The strategy provided in the successive Master Plans has not been able to control market forces, thus leading to an unorganized and haphazard mushrooming of small-scale industries everywhere in the city.[6] Most of these industries cause not only more pollution, but waste material too. Industries are permissible only in the prescribed zones and use premises. However, there are more than one lakh unorganized or informal sector units operating in non-conforming areas such as factory spaces, which are badly maintained. These chemicals, plastics, PVC and electroplating units function in excessively insanitary and unsafe conditions. However, it has not been possible to shift these units from Delhi, even though the Master Plans for the city had recommended shifting of such units and the recommendations of the Master Plans remain on paper.

The periodical surveys on the ambient air quality in the NCR indicate that citizens are being subjected to conditions causing serious health problems. The level of particulate matter (PM) is beyond permissible limits and there is no substantial effort towards mitigating the harmful effects on the population residing in the region. We must try to create as many forests as possible, especially of trees and plants with broad leaves and thick foliage that could act as a carbon sink and stall the entry of dust clouds that make

[6]As per the Master Plan 2021, industries are classified as prohibited and non-prohibited. Industries under the first category shall not be permitted to be set up in Delhi. Areas have been specified for setting up different types of industries. In case an industry is set up in an area not specified for it, it is not conforming to the prescribed norms.

breathing extremely difficult for the vulnerable citizens. In case public land is not available, land may be acquired to create city forests—if not throughout the periphery of the city, then at a depth of around half a kilometre, at least in pockets which would contain dust to a considerable extent. We need to adopt extraordinary measures for the management of environmental issues.

Sanitation determines the quality of life of citizens and is closely linked to planning of habitations, maintenance of roads and the efficiency of drainage network. Sadly, inhabitants seem to be completely unconcerned about the filth around them. The staff engaged by the corporations to maintain sanitation in the city believes that a certain level of insanitation is but natural, without realizing its harmful effects on the health of residents. Creation and maintenance of public urinals is an important area of concern in urban governance, with the lack of sufficient public conveniences cited as one of the primary reasons for air and water pollution. However, even where these conveniences do exist, many still prefer to use open grounds due to mismanagement of the facilities. Although regular sanitation does clear the muck, the volumes are so heavy that the existing capacity just collapses. Street vendors, hawkers and rickshaw-wallahs have nowhere to go in the absence of well-maintained public convenience facilities.

There is a genuine need to create these facilities, particularly for this floating population. Further, markets and bus stands must provide toilet and urinal facilities, particularly for senior citizens and women. All efforts to motivate the corporate sector to take up some of these facilities for maintenance have failed over the years. Even the public-private partnership (PPP) scheme launched by the MCD eventually ended in litigation, as the agencies used the space for display of advertisement and not maintenance of urinals and toilets.

The management of municipal solid waste (MSW) and sewerage systems must be accorded top priority, as with each passing year the quantity of garbage increases. The accumulated garbage at the three existing garbage-dumping sites for the city—Ghazipur (East Delhi), Bhalswa (North Delhi) and Okhla (South Delhi)—is close to 28 million tonnes in an area of about 160 acres.[7] No new sites have been found for this purpose. Meanwhile, the receptacles for temporary storage of garbage or dalaos in colonies remain full, as it takes some time to collect and shift the garbage to the dumping sites. These open dalaos could be converted into underground containers of sufficient capacity to conceal the garbage, which would also keep the areas clean and hygienic.

The city also suffers for want of facilities for disposal of e-waste and demolition waste. Without a proper system in place for the collection and scientific management of e-waste, its various harmful chemical components such as

[7]As per the MCD

lead, cadmium, chromium, etc., dumped with other garbage, can spread toxicity as it accumulates in the soil, water and food. The inhalation of these toxic fumes also poses as a serious health risk. Similarly, construction and demolition (C&D) waste is strewn across the city and chokes surface drains and disrupts traffic, besides being an eyesore on the urban landscape. The management of C&D waste is yet another major concern due to the shortage of dumping sites and prohibitive transportation and disposal costs.

We urgently need adequate processing facilities to remove as well as convert MSW, sewerage waste and C&D waste to socially useful products or services. The segregation of wastes at the household level is an ideal solution, as it would then be possible to easily process the combustible materials for efficient generation of electricity and also to recycle the other wastes such as metals and plastic into various socially useful products. Though such an effort was made in the past, there was no tangible gain from it, as after collecting the wastes in a segregated form, it was randomly dumped at garbage-dumping sites.

Ideally, we should first create processing facilities and then establish a system to receive segregated wastes appropriately. Until then, it would be necessary to establish a pre-processing plant and segregate the organically rich materials, combustible materials and inert substances at the processing sites.

There is a huge gap between the quantity of sewage

being generated and the quantity that can be treated by the Delhi Jal Board (DJB). It is little wonder that the Yamuna resembles a nallah. The Idgah slaughterhouse—the main slaughterhouse in Delhi, set up over a century ago—has also contributed heavily to polluting the river. More than 10,000 animals were slaughtered every day with no arrangements for treatment of effluents that flowed directly into the river.[8] In 2010, the slaughterhouse was shifted to a new location at Ghazipur, equipped with German technology and state-of-the-art facilities, alongside the animal market where around 20,000 animals are accommodated. A rendering plant was also set up close to this slaughterhouse to convert the bodies of dead animals into chicken feed, thereby relieving unwanted pressure on garbage-dumping sites. Earlier, local contractors used to be hired to recover the bodies of dead animals from all over the city; these were then carried to the garbage-dumping sites and de-skinned. The carcasses, however, were left out in the open, which attracted thousands of birds of prey.

Stray animals pose another hazard to traffic and health. The menace created by the city's stray dogs is being successfully addressed by the Animal Birth Control (ABC) Programme of the government. Local bodies are implementing the programme through select non-governmental organizations

---

[8]Anju Sharma, 'Caught by the horns', Down to Earth, 28 June 2015, accessed in June 2019, https://www.downtoearth.org.in/blog/caught-by-the-horns-32028

(NGOs). There is a need to shift the stray animals along the periphery of the city by creating the required infrastructure, i.e, by catering to their requirements of water and feed.

The incongruous urban spaces, unplanned colonies, badly maintained roads, the near absence of an effective drainage system, low-lying areas and inadequate processing facilities for scientific disposal of accumulated wastes at the garbage-dumping sites ensure that insanitary conditions prevail, despite ad hoc solutions provided by the local bodies. All the core elements of the proposed smart city plan could flounder unless urgent corrective steps are taken to allow effortless provision of civic amenities.

The prescriptions so far in the successive Master Plans of the Delhi Development Authority (DDA) are extremely conventional. A steadfast, multipronged approach through a democratic process is needed to not only consolidate investments (both public and private) already made in all civic sectors, but also make coordinated efforts towards creating the right kind of infrastructure for making the city safe, secure and clean. Democratic decision-making, although a slow process, is stable and leads to more durable results, as it is based on consensus; it also practically settles and addresses all societal contradictions. After a detailed appraisal of the strengths, weaknesses, opportunities and threats (SWOT) of the policy so formulated, it should be peremptorily ordered to be implemented by the authorities and agencies. The time has come to find innovative and everlasting solutions to the chronic problems of basic infrastructure that leave the authorities and the agencies red-faced, almost on a daily basis.

POLITICALLY DRIVEN SUCCESS

The exposure and experience I have gained while working as the commissioner of the unified Corporation—a body that handles all the governance issues starting from birth until death of a citizen—does not have any parallel. Each day spent in the Corporation is still fresh in my memory. Every day was eventful, spent amidst officials, representatives of the people, and the citizens. Based on this experience in one of the largest laboratories of civic governance, I have made a sincere effort to advance solutions to civic issues in an urban landscape, with an overarching theme of providing a crisis- and pollution-free environment. The solutions proposed in this book may sound radical or even impractical at times, but they are foolproof and permanent solutions for all times to come, if implemented in the intended letter and spirit and in a phased manner, irrespective of the time factor.

The Delhi Metro is a case in point. Its success, to a large extent, is attributable to a strong political will which cuts across party lines such that even minor issues in the way of execution of the Metro plans received the undivided attention of the highest executives and effective solutions were found, even if it meant amending the rules itself. There is a strong case for the same political will to implement solutions that would make the capital garbage free and also help save the scarce public and natural resources. These solutions need to be created or invented even if the path to achieve them may seem to be full of obstacles and difficulties. I firmly believe that they would work, and facilitate the changes required in the management of environmental issues in the city.

ONE

FLEXING MUSCLE TO AMEND AN INFLEXIBLE WORK ETHIC

When I joined the MCD in the month of February 2008, I was sceptical of what I was going to achieve, going by the public image of the organization as an outrightly inefficient, unresponsive, incorrigible and almost dead body. In fact, some of my colleagues cautioned me to be extra careful and to protect myself, as the organization was considered to be a 'kajal ki kothari' (i.e. a room of black kohl) and anybody who worked within was bound to be stained, regardless of whether one engaged in any dark practice or not. Others encouraged me to take on the assignment as a challenge and an opportunity to contribute positively in the governance of India's capital city.

In any case, I was quite excited to read about my appointment as the commissioner, MCD, when it first appeared as breaking news on television channels. It gave me a unique sense of pride and fulfilment, as it was an important appointment. There was an uppity politician who asked whether I had approached anyone to get the order of appointment, and wanted to know who that person was. I found it quite unsettling and strange, as I too had seen the news being telecast on television the previous day for the first time. My eldest brother was almost taken over by ecstasy when he heard of the appointment. For him, having guided me as a college student and thereafter, to see me join the Indian Administrative Service (IAS) was a moment of pride. For me, too, it was the fittest way to serve the nation as a part of the Service that had helped to build and keep the country integrated. I had hopes and aspirations, as well as mixed feelings of happiness and nervousness, for the challenges ahead of me. After having served the unified MCD for more than four years, I felt nothing could have been more satisfying than serving the second-largest municipal corporation of the world. Also, the rumours and unsavoury stories about the Corporation spread by vested interests need to be discarded. In an organization like the MCD, certain negative elements inevitably bring disrepute due to the very nature of services and regulatory control that its officers are required to provide and enforce. The only solution is to bring in transparency in the working of the Corporation, which was attempted with great effort and success. The easy availability of municipal services without having to visit the offices of the local body, i.e. without any interface with officials, would help to reduce corrupt practices.

Soon after taking over, while addressing the press about my priorities, I promised transparency in the working of the Corporation as the key to deliver hassle-free service, which would ultimately help to eradicate corruption from the Corporation. It is now a matter of record that the e-Governance initiative of the Corporation, implemented since 2010, ushered in a system of service delivery free from corruption of any kind. However, the subsequent trifurcation of the Corporation into the North Delhi Municipal Corporation, the South Delhi Municipal Corporation and the East Delhi Municipal Corporation killed all the initiatives, as they were designed for the unified Corporation. The decision to trifurcate the unified MCD was practically an unilateral decision taken without consulting the stakeholders. The decision makers probably thought that the smaller local bodies would be more responsive, efficient and self-reliant without considering the socio-economic potential of each area and their interdependence for various activities, services, etc. The result is for everyone to see. The South Delhi Corporation is able to mop up sufficient revenue, whereas the East and North Corporations are always struggling to pay wages and the salaries to the staff.

The unified Corporation with its 1,75,000 personnel in thirty-nine-odd departments was spread across the entire territory of the city, barring the areas under the jurisdiction of the NDMC and the DCB, which together occupy an area measuring only about 82 sq. km, i.e., 6 per cent of the total area of the union territory of Delhi.

The most important consideration lay in the fact that the jurisdiction of the unified MCD serviced 97 per cent of the population in the territory, and in some of the most difficult, inaccessible areas—in the sense that the civic body provided sanitary services to areas not connected by roads. The atmosphere of work in a Corporation of this size, spread and reach is bound to be upbeat and dynamic due to its very nature, yet it is bridled by officers reporting late for work, long winding processes, project delays, unaddressed public grievances and even corruption. Nothing that approachability and a dose of discipline cannot tackle.

OPEN DOOR POLICY

The first day after taking charge gave me a clear idea of things to expect on a regular basis: the stream of visitors, regular meetings with the elected representatives, among others. I set the rules of the game. Anyone could meet the commissioner and officers anytime—there was no need to make an appointment. The objective was to allow an atmosphere of free flow of information. This entailed a tight schedule and stretching of office hours for file work. This, I thought, was necessary, as citizens and employees must have a platform to express their feelings or grievances. The information and grievances thus received also needed to be followed through and acted upon on a daily basis, to be taken to their logical settlement.

This was certainly not to the liking of many who had gotten used to settling these matters superficially. For others, this was a sort of intrusion in their exclusive domain where they dictated the manner and the kind of redressal, which had a balanced equation of give and take. The response from the general public, however, was positive. The councillors who could meet the commissioner without any prior appointment and without any restriction and got the legitimate work done without any delay became willing partners in the crusade against corruption of any form and manner.

To take openness to the next level, it was decided that the Corporation officers would gather in formal weekly meetings. When the private secretary (PS) to the commissioner was told to fix the meeting at 10.00 in the morning, he politely advised me to fix the meeting at 11.00, as apparently nobody would come for a meeting that early. When he was asked to fix the meeting at 9.00 a.m., he gently retorted saying that the meeting should be fixed for 8.30

a.m. instead. When I confirmed the time as 8.30 a.m., the PS looked at me, unable to believe that his advice would take the meeting to what was clearly an unearthly hour. Senior officers assembled on time and after formal introductions, strategies to tackle the various issues confronting the Corporation were discussed. It is a matter of record that during my tenure in the Corporation spanning over four years, barring a few occasions, the weekly meetings were regularly held every Tuesday at 8.30 in the morning.

Regular meetings were also initiated with the people's representatives—the Members of the Legislative Assembly (MLAs) and the Members of Parliament (MPs)—in the presence of the residents of their areas. These meetings were always fruitful, as they focussed on the genuine difficulties and problems requiring delivery of services or solutions without delay. Such meetings were held as a matter of routine. The minutes of the meetings were drawn up the same day and circulated among all officers for reporting action in the weekly meetings held every Tuesday morning. The results were rewarding, as regular reviews of the decisions ensured their timely and effective implementation.

As I learnt later, it was the first time that heads of different departments became privy to the happenings in other departments and in the local wards, which was, in any case, required for better coordination and effective supervision. The regular meetings gave us an opportunity to review the progress in the implementation of schemes, disposal of public grievances and current issues that warranted close monitoring. Officers became wary, as any delays were to be explained in the presence of other officers. Fearing embarrassment and loss of face, officers took personal care in ensuring timely redressal of the grievances. The good and efficient delivery of services by the officers was appreciated in full measure, and the results were rewarding too.

The next step was to set time targets as yet another instrument for checking delays in responding to letters and grievances received from the offices of the lieutenant governor (LG), chief minister (CM) or the Government of India. A small section, comprising two persons, was set up in the personal branch of the commissioner to diarize in a separate register the receipt of important letters marked as 'M' reference by the commissioner, and with follow-up action for timely disposal. Instructions were issued separately to dispose of the references within fifteen days, with any unexplained delay leading to appropriate action against the official concerned. This, I found, was an effective tool in facilitating expeditious disposal of references and settlement of public grievances, permanently and quickly.

Even internal grievances within the MCD family were expeditiously resolved. On one occasion, the wife of a deceased ex-employee met me in the office. She informed me that her husband had worked in the Corporation and died seven years ago, just before his retirement, and she was still running from pillar to post to get his dues. Checking the information collated from all the departments of the Corporation revealed that there were more than 700 cases pending final disposal—in some cases for as long as seven years—and as discovered subsequently, for reasons which could at best be described as bizarre. It was then decided that the entire dues to the retiring employees would be paid on the very day of their retirement. Each department was required to issue a notification, every month, of the employees due to retire in the next six months to facilitate completion of all the formalities. The departmental heads or Deputy Commissioners (DCs) of the zones were directed to personally ensure that the formalities were fast-tracked, and any difficulty encountered by the DCs was to be raised in the weekly meetings for appropriate resolution.

PUTTING THE BRAKES ON WASTEFUL EXPENDITURE

As the commissioner, I was responsible for the collection of revenue from all possible sources, to make the organization self-reliant and reduce dependence on outside help to perform the obligatory functions. I soon found that one of the most popular activities in the Corporation was the inauguration and laying of foundation stones of buildings, parks and other such projects. There would be a huge rush, particularly towards the end of the financial year, to organize such functions. This would entail not only the cost of the stone or the metallic plaque, but other related expenditures too, such as the printing of invitation cards, erecting the shamiana with furniture arrangements, and organizing snacks, lunch or dinner. Each function cost the Corporation anything between ₹20,000–₹50,000 or even more in some cases depending on the status of the VIP invited for the ceremony.

The money spent on such activities, which took place almost every month in almost all the 272 wards of the twelve zones of the Corporation, added up to a few crores every year. This, I felt, was wasteful expenditure causing a clear dent on the hard-earned revenue of the Corporation, given the state of its finances. However, efforts to curb these ceremonies had little impact. Discontinuing such activities could save a lot of money, enough to strengthen the infrastructure needed to provide educational and healthcare facilities in the city.

There was another striking source of excess related to payments being made for public work that was not carried out appropriately. The Corporation's personnel, known as nallah beldars, were hired to clean the drains in the city. They had been working in the Corporation over the years but had largely forgotten the duty they were recruited for and shifted to white collar jobs in air-conditioned rooms, with hardly any work worth its name. They were supposed to keep the nallahs clog free throughout the year, and with around 2,200 of them, it should have been ensured year after year that the rainwater and waste water drains are blockage free, by removing the silt from nallahs on a regular basis. The workers were, however, not there, and lo and behold, the work of desilting of the nallahs was contracted out. The contractors, however, were hardly interested in desilting the nallahs and the overflows were but natural.

A letter arrived at my office in March 2008 informing that the contractors assigned the job of desilting the nallahs were actually getting their payments by collecting slips from the weighbridges at the landfill sites for depositing C&D waste (other than silt) collected from private land in the city and even from outside the city. The personnel manning the weighbridges at the landfill sites were not checking what was being brought in. So, the contractors enjoyed a windfall payment from the Corporation on the basis of these slips and also from those constructing or reconstructing their houses or shops, and from those required to deposit demolition waste at the landfill sites.

The action taken thereafter to rectify the situation led to a kind of uproar, with many in the Corporation arguing that the nallah beldars had got used to working in the offices and it would, therefore, be unfair to put them back on the same job. Despite the opposition, the nallah beldars were asked to report at the sites and all the contracts for desilting the nallahs were cancelled. The situation thereafter improved as close monitoring of the desilting work was done at the highest executive level in the Corporation throughout the year, not only at the desk but also on the ground all over the city.

This demonstrates the kind of loss caused to the public exchequer in a case where no one was accountable and the Corporation was paying around ₹22 crore as the salary annually to the nallah beldars (approx. 2,200 of them) in 2008 while the work that they were required to do was contracted out, thus involving a cost of around ₹25–₹30 crore per annum.

One more area of profligacy was the supply of flowers on a daily basis by a private agency to the chambers of all the officers and councillors in the Corporation. I was puzzled. While I agreed that flowers could make the officers and councillors feel good, particularly in the otherwise-insipid environment of the Corporation, I wondered why the Horticulture Department of the Corporation, which had substantial staff strength, was not considered capable of providing these flowers. This arrangement, I found, was costing the Corporation an enormous amount of money—with no perceptible difference on the faces of the officers and councillors. They still wore the same look throughout the day, which was a given considering the nature of their work. The contract with the agency responsible for supplying the flowers was cancelled forthwith. Officers were given the option of arranging for the flowers on their own through the good offices of the personnel in the Department of Horticulture, which maintained quite a few nurseries. I feel that contrived happiness is no substitute for the happiness that comes naturally from a job well done.

Another insidious expense I identified was the enormous wastage of paper on a daily basis. It was eating into the vitals of the Corporation. The meetings of various committees and the House of the Corporation required circulation of the agenda to all the councillors and officers in advance. Such notices could easily be circulated by getting an appropriate application customized for the communication, such as through apps like Whatsapp or via email. All the reports of the actions taken could also be circulated through that application. Even a one-time investment in technical aid for communication is a feasible idea. Although an initiative was taken, there was reluctance by the councillors to follow through, as most of them were not computer friendly. Hence, it was no surprise that following the trifurcation, the e-Governance project encountered a serious stumbling block. Yet, the saving of paper in the Corporation would have a direct bearing on the environment and also help to combat the ill effects of pollution.

ENFORCING DISCIPLINE

One factor at the core of efficiency in any public office is the punctuality of the officials. It facilitates the availability of the municipal services without any waste of time. However, the habit of coming late to office and then not being available in the appropriate section was not new in the Corporation. It was endemic, with one significant exception. Since sanitation and other essential services are looked after by the Corporation, it cannot brook delays. Garbage not lifted regularly is an eyesore and any delay would cause the litter to pile up, with stray animals spreading it further—thus causing bad odour in the area, hindering walking spaces, creating an unhygienic environment and being a health risk. The workforce is, therefore, required to be deployed in their respective areas with regularity and on time.

The safai karamcharis (sweepers), malis, domestic breeding checkers, malaria beldars and other field workers in the Corporation account for a sizeable number in the overall strength of the organization, and when expressed in terms of the percentage of the total staff strength, it should be around 70–80 per cent. A sizeable amount of money is set apart in the total budget of the Corporation for their salaries and wages. Moreover, the services they provide are under public scrutiny on a daily basis. They can make or mar the image of the local body.

So, even as we were dealing with punctuality among employees, an old friend, a professor in one of the universities in Delhi, asked me if the Corporation allowed its employees to work elsewhere in addition to their duties in the Corporation. This was quite startling and on making inquiries, it became clear that there were indeed grey areas in the attendance of the staff that needed to be corrected.

It was decided to put into place a foolproof system bereft of manual involvement, which could automatically ensure that the status of attendance is appraised regularly. Anyone found not attending the place of duty could be prosecuted as per the extant office rules. We introduced a pilot project for the implementation of a system of biometric attendance for the sanitation staff of the Paharganj zone. The staff was livid. The office bearers of the union of the safai karamcharis of the MCD looked upon this proposal as discriminatory and threatened to go on strike in protest against the pilot project. The proposal was put on hold.

However, after careful consideration of various factors and the possible fallout of any such move, it was thought appropriate to implement the pilot project for the headquarter (HQ) offices located at Delhi Town Hall and Ambedkar Stadium. The system became operational on 1 August 2008 and ushered in a new era of punctuality in the Corporation. Now one could see queues of employees waiting to mark their attendance by putting their forefingers on the sensors in the biometric machines. But the marking of attendance while coming in the morning and again at the time of departure from office obviously did not impress everyone.

For instance, a lower-level employee had once dipped his finger in oil before marking his attendance. The oil disabled the sensor and it could not be used to capture the identity of the employee. Another employee scratched the sensor with his nail, which again disabled the sensor. Some officers wanted to be exempted from marking their attendance, as they were required to go to court. All such requests were turned down and employees were asked to first come to the office before going out into the field. If there was indeed a requirement to go to court or any other office for a meeting and it was not practical to attend office first, these officers were directed to take prior approval from the commissioner. Staff that meddled with the machines was apprehended and departmental proceedings were initiated against them, leading to major penalties. The message was loud and clear. Discipline was non-negotiable. All employees were required to be punctual and regular in attending office. Moreover, as the commissioner himself regularly and religiously marked his attendance, employees had no choice but to comply with the orders.

Some employees tried a different tack to subvert the system. They reported to office on time but after marking their attendance, went missing and reappeared again at the time of departure. The Chief Vigilance Officer (CVO) was asked to constitute attendance-checking squads to randomly check the physical presence of the employees, and anyone found missing after marking their attendance was proceeded against under the provisions of the conduct rules for dereliction of duty. The payment of salaries and wages was also digitally linked to the biometric attendance system. It took nearly a month to settle the glitches, and for the system to work as planned. It paid rich dividends, as all employees were available in their position—so much so that even on days when there was a call for 'Bharat Bandh', the employees of the Corporation were there in their offices well on time. The work culture underwent a definite change for the better. Citizens did not have to wait unnecessarily to get their work done, as employees were present.

Following the success of the pilot project, the biometric attendance system was implemented in a phased manner to cover all the offices throughout the territory and also for those working in the field, such as safai karamcharis, malis, etc. Field formations (i.e. sites where employees or workers like malis, sweepers, etc. report for duties) were covered by mobile biometric machines that were carried by the supervisory staff. However, when the supervisory staff started to maliciously interfere with the machines, the DCs of the Corporation were strictly instructed to recover the cost of the machines from the salary of the supervisory officers concerned and in case a DC failed to do so, the cost was to be recovered from the salary of the DC himself. This veiled threat ensured that no machine was deliberately spoiled by anyone.

The successful implementation of the system required regular monitoring at the highest level. The machines were programmed to transmit the information on real-time basis, so it was possible to find out the number of employees working in the various offices scattered all over the territory.

It took about six months to complete the implementation of the system to cover all the offices of the Corporation. The implementation of the biometric system of attendance was a welcome step, as it brought the required discipline. Sincere employees—those who were punctual and regular in attending to their duties—felt happy to see their habitually erring colleagues come to office on time. This, in turn, led to improved employee efficiency.

However, serious logistical difficulties were encountered during the implementation of the biometric attendance scheme, as technology took some time to weed out the deep-seated rot. For preparing the baseline data, all the employees were required to provide the impression of their forefingers and their particulars for cross verification. There were around 25,000 employees constantly defying all instructions for registration, as they thought they could get away with defiance and continue to follow the age-old system in which they would come to office only to collect their wages and salaries once in several months—or even six months in some cases.

The absence of any employee on leave for even a short duration could create a problem in dispensing essential services such as sanitation. Therefore, successive dispensations in the Corporation allowed the supervisory officers to hire another employee in their place till the regular employee returned from leave. Such workers who worked during the leave period of an employee came to be known as substitute employees, and this arrangement was made in all the wards throughout the city.

Supervisory officers, in course of time, had innovated a system of sending the regular employees on leave by turns and keeping substitute employees. The substitute employees were physically sent back after a few days, but they continued to work on paper as their details were captured in the record. Their wages were drawn and deposited in their accounts that were opened and operated by the supervisory officers. Regular employees were advised to remain on leave (unauthorized) by turns and supervisory officers would draw the wages of both the regular as well as substitute employees, and keep half with themselves. The supervisory officers had perfected this system over the years by maintaining duplicate, concurrent records in their private offices, manned by privately engaged employees.

The system suited the supervisory officers as well as the regular employees who were on leave by turns, and the wages drawn in the names of substitute employees were shared between them in some proportion to the quantum of risk taken by them. Regular employees received their full salary and when on leave, the employees substituted in their places were shown to have been paid wages. The introduction of the biometric system of attendance put an end to this gross violation of rules of conduct. The system necessitated the verification of employee details and payment was to be made by the disbursing officer directly into the accounts of the employees, whether regular or substitute. Therefore, it was no longer possible to continue with the old system of paying the substitute employees only on paper.

When information of 25,000 employees who were not providing the impression of their forefingers became public, the newspapers termed it as the curious case of the ghost employees, with front page reports in the national dailies covering the colossal loss to the exchequer of hundreds of crores every year on account of the existence of these ghost employees. The news spread like wild fire and there was almost an upheaval in the Corporation; a case was registered against the unknown and bogus employees.

In another case, a fake order was issued transferring two dozen safai karamcharis not on the rolls of the Corporation from one zone to another. The officers of the zone to which they were transferred allowed them to join duty even without checking their antecedents. The system was so well perfected that no one got any hint of these doings in the Corporation. It, therefore, took a long time for the mischief to be discovered and remedial action to be taken as per the provisions of the relevant law.

The overall monetary benefit from the introduction of disciplinary measures and the biometric attendance system may be difficult to guess, but it would easily be hundreds of crores every year even by a crude method of estimation. Besides saving man-days, the system made it possible to ensure attendance of workers and employees at their respective workstations. The improvement in work efficiency throughout the city was perceptible.

It is my experience that once the reins are let loose, the rot seeps in and ultimately the employees tend to slip back into their comfort zones. The requirement, therefore, is to cultivate a system of monitoring and close supervision at all levels and at all times, with no compromise on the working hours and quality of work.

TWO

UNEASY ALLIANCES: A TIGHTROPE WALK

'Being a civil servant is like walking on a tightrope over a deep valley.' I remember these words of the chief secretary of a state where I was under training during my formative years. He believed that any mistake in performing one's duties could take them down to unfathomable depths. Later, I would vouch for this statement from personal experience—especially when as a commissioner appointed by the Ministry of Home Affairs (MHA), I was accountable to the Central Government and was working with councillors, representing the local government and being responsible to the state government. Being accountable at all levels of the government while leading one of the world's largest municipal bodies, with jurisdiction over more than 94 per cent of Delhi and providing civic services for a population of over 16 million people, was certainly complex. And it became trickier still when in 2011 the Central Government delegated some of its powers over the MCD to the state government.

The Legislative Assembly of the National Capital Territory (NCT) of Delhi amended the Delhi Municipal Corporation Act, 1957, which had the effect of splitting the MCD into three smaller bodies on 13 January 2012. Thus, a united MCD was trifurcated into the North Delhi Municipal Corporation and South Delhi Municipal Corporation, each covering 104 municipal wards, and the smaller East Delhi Municipal Corporation, having jurisdiction over sixty-four wards. Each municipal ward elects a councillor, who is like a bridge between the community and the Corporation, and represents a political party and the ward on the municipal Corporation.

This amendment also brought in state-level involvement in the local bodies with the secretary of Urban Development in the Delhi government designated as the director of the local bodies, with the responsibility of overseeing the three municipal corporations.

Being accountable at all levels of the government was a tightrope walk and a test of courage and balance, as the initiatives of the Corporation were always looked down upon by even the lower-level functionaries in the government.

No one believed that a number of reforms, including e-Governance, had been successfully implemented by the MCD. The general (and of course, wrong) impression in the government is that many activities in the Corporation are carried out without following rules and without maintaining proper records. The happenings in the Corporation were not very different from what may take place elsewhere in the state government or the Central Government or even in the Department of Space!

It was common knowledge that the ruling political parties played host to their own members when they should be impartial in matters in the public domain. For instance, rules were provided for equitable allocation of funds to all organizations based on a formula decided by the Finance Commission. However, those in control of allocation of funds ensured the release of legitimate funds at a belated stage when there was little time left to utilize them, and this was orchestrated as non-performance and made the basis of all arguments against funding for the local body.

ULTERIOR POLITICAL MOTIVES AND LOSS OF FAITH

Often, the Corporation was caught between the offices of the governments at the state and the Centre. I have vivid memories of a meeting held in the chamber of a senior union minister to decide the allocation of funds from the corpus of the Urban Development Fund (UDF) maintained by the DDA. The money in the corpus comes as a certain percentage of the bid amount given by successful bidders participating in the bidding process for allotment of land, etc.

It struck me one day that three roads in Delhi, namely Najafgarh to Dhansa Border, Najafgarh to Uttam Nagar and Najafgarh to Nangloi had one thing in common—they were dotted with potholes throughout the year. The patchy repair work only worsened this condition, as with the onset of rains, the potholes at these stretches grew deeper. The volume of traffic on all three roads was growing fast every year too. The roads had constructional faults for entire stretches with no side drains. In addition, agricultural fields accompanied the roads for substantial lengths. A solution was urgently needed to help keep the roads motorable throughout the year. The Delhi government had given a proposal to repair the road from Najafgarh to Dhansa Border, but that, however, did not materialize even after the Corporation had given the formal permission.

I had heard of the roller compacted concrete (RCC) road constructed along the coast in Mumbai that was able to successfully withstand the fury of floods, which were accentuated by storms in the sea. Although the cost of building such a road would be higher, it would be offset by almost no requirement of maintenance for at least fifteen to twenty years, unless the road is cut off mechanically for laying down pipelines for public utilities and so on.

I approached the secretary of the Ministry of Surface Transport to help the local body relay the road on this stretch. This would facilitate the development of the rural areas of western Delhi, which almost serves as the hinterland for the urbanized areas of Delhi. The secretary was gracious enough to treat this as a special case and sanctioned a grant for the requisite amount, for which a proposal was submitted to the Ministry of Surface Transport.

The news of the grant reached the officers of the Delhi government, who briefed the minister concerned. He was visibly annoyed and insisted that the road would be repaired by the Delhi government irrespective of the grant being sanctioned by the Government of India. I informed him that since the work had not yet been taken up for almost eighteen months since the granting of permission to the Flood Control Department in the Delhi government, it may not be possible for the Corporation to sustain the permission, particularly after the funds had arrived from the Government of India. I also explained to him that the funds of the Delhi government could be used elsewhere, as even patch repairs would just be half-done with an amount of ₹10 crore—the amount they were sparing for the road. The Government of India had, on the other hand, sanctioned ₹65 crore and that amount could facilitate converting the road from blacktopped to RCC. The minister reluctantly agreed, and the road was relaid as planned. It is now a treat to the eyes, with compliments pouring in from almost everybody who uses that road.

After receiving the grant for the Najafgarh-Dhansa Border road, it was proposed to acquire similar grants for the roads from Najafgarh to Nangloi and from Najafgarh to Uttam Nagar. A proposal was accordingly prepared and forwarded to the Ministry of Urban Development through the Government of Delhi to get the funds sanctioned by the UDF, operated by the DDA. The funds from the UDF are sanctioned by a committee comprising the LG and CM of Delhi, amongst others, and the committee is headed by the Union Urban Development minister. The meeting was fixed in the chamber of the Union Urban Development minister. All the members, including the CM and the LG of Delhi, were present. I attended the meeting as a representative of the MCD, as the proposals were required to be formally explained to the committee.

Meanwhile, I had heard that following the successful implementation of the Najafgarh to Dhansa Border Project, stakeholders were eager to grab political mileage from a success story—a story of the development of the area that they banked on during the campaigning of the municipal elections, which were then round the corner.

The committee soon approved the grant of funds for the two proposals, but with a rider. The chairman of the Committee (i.e. the Union Urban Development minister) announced that the projects would be implemented not by the MCD but by the Public Works Department (PWD) of the Government of Delhi. The chairman further clarified that the decision had been taken because they did not consider the engineers of the MCD competent enough to execute the projects properly and efficiently.

I was shocked when the minister stated in a meeting that the officers of the local body were not competent enough to execute the projects, when it was the MCD engineers who had put in time and effort to prepare the detailed proposal. I explained to him that the MCD engineers were as competent as the engineers of any other department and enumerated the examples of various projects successfully completed by the MCD, such as the Civic Centre, etc. But no argument could convince the minister. The project was shifted from the MCD to the PWD, Government of Delhi.

Anyway, the reasons for the twist in the story were not too hard to find. The political party in power at the Centre was also the ruling party in the Government of Delhi. A different party was, however, in power in the MCD. The argument of the minister in stating that the engineers of the MCD were not competent enough was possibly a ploy to pass on the projects to the PWD. This was done perhaps in order to benefit the party from the constituency where the projects were to be implemented. However, the manner in which such a decision was taken was not in good taste, as the entire MCD was shown in a bad light.

The Corporation had, in fact, initiated a process of major reforms encompassing all facets of its working, and far from appreciating its bold efforts, the organization was being treated shabbily. This is the kind of attitude that perhaps all political parties have, as they tend to favour their own members and interests. This needs to change. What happened to the political mileage of the party concerned, for whom such a decision was taken? The same political party came back to power in the Corporation! Fraud and intimidation were also used as tools of political corruption.

POLITICAL PRESSURES

I had another nerve-wracking experience. A person approached me through an ex-union minister under whom I had worked during my deputation to the Central Government. The ex-minister spoke to me over the phone and asked me to help the poor fellow, as he had been running from pillar to post without any success. I assured the minister that I would personally look into the matter and get it settled expeditiously. Little did I know then that the matter was not so simple, as it had elements of fraud and conspiracy in collusion with a serving government servant!

The request of the applicant, who also happened to be a politician, was to allow him possession of a public park in West Delhi, as it had been wrongly developed as a park by the MCD. I found the request quite unusual, as the local body could not have invested huge funds to develop a private plot of land into a public park. He, however, had in his possession documents to prove his claim. On perusal, the documents appeared genuine and there was no reason to doubt them. However, a formal inquiry was made to establish his claim.

The matter was examined in the office and a recommendation was made to hand over possession of the public park to him. Yet, I dragged my feet as I strongly believed that the Corporation would not have invested public funds into private land. I wanted the whole matter to be thoroughly investigated in consultation with officers of the DDA. In case it was private land, who had authorized the officers to invest public funds for the development of a public park? The need to fix the responsibility of the officers who had wasted public funds weighed heavily on my mind. The matter was examined by a different set of officers. Even they did not find time to go into the depth of the matter, and recommended the possession of the public park to be handed over. The file was put up to me for approval. I was still not convinced.

Meanwhile, the applicant approached the National Commission for Scheduled Castes (NCSC) and filed an application for the issuance of appropriate direction to me to hand over possession of the land to him. The commission summoned a few DDA officers and me to appear before its chairman—an ex-IAS officer and an MP—and explain why the possession of the land was not being handed over. I appeared before the commission and explained that the land could not have been developed into a public park in case it was private property. The chairman of the commission made caustic observations and lambasted the officers of the Corporation for adopting a casual approach in dealing with such sensitive cases that involved the rights of a person from a scheduled caste. I requested the commission to allow me some time to prove my position in larger public interest, and also to ensure that no wrong was done to anybody and certainly not to a common man. The chairman allowed me time on the condition that it would be the last opportunity and that the officers concerned would face serious consequences in case they did not file the requisite report in the stipulated time. The officers of the Corporation and those from the DDA attending the hearing were worried because, based on the documents available with the applicant, there was no way he could be proved wrong. They also thought that my assumption of the land being acquired was simply wishful thinking. I was, however, confident that the land had been acquired and handed over to the Corporation for development as a public park.

A team was constituted to visit the office of the DDA to find whether the piece of land in question in that particular khasra number of the revenue estate of the village had ever been acquired and if yes, whether it was officially handed over to the MCD for development as a public park.

It was an exercise in digging up old records. The DDA officers who had attended the hearings of the commission were helpful. Finally, following a search that extended for two to three days, we could lay our hands on the relevant documents, buried deep in the record room. All the officers were relieved that ultimately the documents relating to the acquisition of the land had been found and they were all spared from taking an illegal decision that would have become serious. If the DDA officers had taken the pains and found the old records earlier, the matter would not have reached the commission in the first place. The right hand in the DDA did not seem to know what the left hand was doing. The documents clearly revealed that the acquisition of that particular piece of land was done in the mid-'60s and was later on handed over to the Corporation for development as a public park. The documents in the possession of the applicant seemed to have been issued by a lower-level functionary in the DDA in collusion with the applicant.

When the report was presented in the commission, the chairman had the audacity to comment that it was false and that he was thinking of referring the matter to the Central Bureau of Investigation (CBI) for fixing responsibility, as a member of the scheduled castes was being denied possession of land owned by him. The chairman fixed another date and insisted that the commissioner should be personally present to depose further in the matter. A summons was issued against me. The chairman seemed hell-bent on harassing me, who had unearthed a fraud with far-reaching implications. The Government of Delhi had to be requested to give permission to file a case in the High Court of Delhi for staying the summons issued against me. It was a clear case of overreach by the commission to investigate a matter that was essentially to be decided by the revenue authorities. The High Court stayed the summons and prima facie found merit in the grounds that the particular piece of land was public. The officials who had issued fake documents to the applicant went unpunished. Each day, I would mount the tightrope, careful about not making mistakes.

AN UNWELCOME GIFT

Attempts by the councillors to find fault with anybody who mattered was quite common. The junior-level officers of the Corporation who were close to them, obviously for their own interests and protection, were their 'watch eyes'.

I was once invited to declare a newly constructed school open for use. The local councillor from the opposition party, to express his happiness on his performance, presented me with a gold chain on the dais. The occasion and the place were so solemn that I found it inappropriate to say no. The gift should not have been given nor accepted, as it was totally uncalled for and it certainly was not the right way of honouring anybody. It was rather a kind of insult to the system and the public offices occupied by both of us. The matter was dutifully reported by the 'watch eyes' to the political masters, who planned to organize a sort of coup d'état against the commissioner.

Meanwhile, no sooner did I return to my office than I officially reported the episode to the chief secretary, the CM and the LG in writing stating that I had politely returned the gold chain to the councillor. The plan of the leaders of the ruling party to raise the issue in the ensuing meeting of the House floundered when they learnt that I had intimated the whole incident to the higher authorities and also returned the gift. In retrospect, I sincerely regret that I had accepted the gift—which was a mistake, as any such offer should have been declined publicly and politely right there and then. In all fairness to some members of the ruling party in the Corporation, it needs to be mentioned that they did not approve of the political plotting of the incident with a view to maligning my reputation.

There were a number of similar occasions when some of the councillors, unable to get their way, tried repeatedly to browbeat and tyrannize me on one pretext or another. They would shout slogans against the commissioner and even carry slogans on wooden 'takhties' (boards) tied to their chests. Such demonstrations were held to indicate that the commissioner should mend his ways, or else they would up the ante and make it difficult for him to function in the Corporation. Motives of the councillors were usually governed by their affiliation to a political party rather than public issues, as was on display in the meetings of the House.

A MINI PARLIAMENT

To work closely on public issues at all levels mandated participation in the proceedings, particularly of the Standing Committee and the House of the Corporation. (The House of the Corporation comprises all the elected representatives known as the councillors, and meets at least once a month or as necessary to discuss and elicit the members' views on issues of larger public interest.) The Standing Committee has the mandate to scrutinize all the proposals prepared by the commissioner on the various public issues relating to all its thirty-nine departments. It also has the power to process and approve the proposals involving the utilization of funds for the various schemes and programmes of the Corporation. The approval, however, is subject to the final concurrence of the House of the Corporation.

The councillors representing the ruling party participate in the discussions and toe the party line, garnishing the achievements of the party with narrative embellishments. The councillors of the opposition parties generally criticize the decisions on one pretext or another, calling the claims of the ruling party acts of braggadocio. There are also situations when all parties unite to support a cause in larger public interest, but that happens rarely. The participants of the discussions in the House represent the voices of the people who elected them and in that sense, the House is like a mini Parliament. The pugnacious nature of some of the councillors vitiates the otherwise subtle environment of the sessions.

Most members of the House participated in the discussions with all seriousness, as they were genuinely concerned about the issues and endeavoured to find solutions to the woes of the citizens. Many members exhibited erudition on subjects that could seem esoteric and difficult to comprehend. But one could see through the machinations of the various groups working with vested interest and lobbying to get some projects approved.

ULTERIOR MOTIVES

Lobbying was common for moving proposals. There was one retired, avuncular official who, after being in the Corporation for more than four decades in a particular department, was working as the éminence grise of a political heavyweight. He knew the tricks of getting a proposal approved or rejected on technical grounds. He seemed to have a sound knowledge of the procedures and practices of the committees and the House, and therefore, was much sought after by many politicians who were beginners in the Corporation. He was also equally useful to unscrupulous elements, inside as well as outside the Corporation, in blocking many projects that were useful for the general public on the ground that these did not suit their requirements.

It was no wonder then, that several initiatives taken to streamline and enhance revenue collected from parking and display of advertisements were always checkmated with the assistance of a few councillors, who were helping an established syndicate of rapacious contractors. And in case any breakthroughs were achieved, they were killed by dragging the Corporation to court on some ground or the other. All those involved in these deals perhaps practiced a code of omertà, as they succeeded most of the time.

The lessons learnt from these failures clearly indicated one thing—that officials are not trained to draft agreements, whereas professionals engaged by unscrupulous contractors could ensure that any gaps could be eventually used by unscrupulous elements to their advantage. The Corporation would lose revenue and the contractors and their chuffed cronies would make merry, and no one could find out the deals made between them, as everything would occur within the framework of the prescribed procedure.

These professionals could even compel the Corporation to continue with a contract by default, just because it could not be legally renewed for some time due to the local body having accepted a seemingly innocuous proposal on some ordinary pretext. For example, I remember an overbearing councillor with an imperious air in an important position lobbying for some contracts to be continued for one more month. Doing that would eventually force the Corporation to continue with the contract on the same terms and conditions, and sometimes even at the same rates. In this case, since the contract period was going to be over, efforts were made to somehow stretch it further. In case the project was re-contracted, the payment to be made to the Corporation would double. The continuation of the contract, even for a few more months, would help them earn much more. Many of the officials, even at senior levels, are too naïve and sometimes callow to fathom the depth and real purpose of such lobbying. The story has been told and retold all these years on the same wavelengths. What could be more egregious than those elected by the public to protect the interests of the Corporation eating into the vitals of the organization?

Truly, the councillors, unmindful of the role of the commissioner as defined in the governing act of the Parliament, felt they had supremacy in the working of the Corporation. For example, revenue collection from all possible sources is one of the primary responsibilities of the commissioner. However, while the elected representatives always spoke about the need of making the Corporation self-reliant, this was only public rhetoric. All the councillors would speak against the collection of property tax from unauthorized colonies and villages, but in the next breath, expect all civic facilities to be extended to these areas. This is certainly a contradiction in terms and I strongly feel that all the political parties should rise above their sole target of winning elections entirely through offering concessions.

PRESSURES OF NEPOTISM AND CORRUPTION

I was called into a meeting where the then mayor made a request, presumably on behalf of all the councillors. The mayor stated without mincing his words that I could buy permanent peace with the councillors if one or two persons per councillor were appointed by me as per their advice—as was done by all previous commissioners who had been making such appointments. The request was repeated by the mayor over a period of about four or five months. This I thought was a unique way of perhaps cosseting the elected members that involved creating a regular and perhaps permanent dent on the earnings of the Corporation. This is because if such appointments are made, even when there is no requirement, the wages or salaries to such appointees will drain the Corporation's earnings. That is an absolute wastage of funds without any gain, year after year till their retirement. The appointments in the Corporation are based on the job requirement and not merely to keep peace amongst functionaries. Why should there be any such requirement of mollycoddling anybody for peace?

In another startling case, a senior councillor reportedly called an executive of a company and told him that he would accept their sanitary equipment only if they paid him ₹5 crore. The company, thereafter, was not interested in dealing with the Corporation. This particular councillor was in the habit of issuing veiled threats to the officers if they did not obey his bidding and it was, therefore, but natural that such posturing by the councillors affected the morale of the officers and their efficiency suffered to some extent. But one particular area in which the councillors and officers were mostly united, with very few exceptions, was against officers on deputation to the Corporation.

Appointments in the Corporation on deputation from other departments of the Delhi government or the Government of India always met with voices of dissonance from the officials as well as (in almost all cases) the elected representatives in the Corporation. I tried to find the main reason for this opposition.

As a matter of principle, it is considered useful to bring in officials from different streams with a view to pooling their expertise and experience to further provide efficient civic services. Even in the Government of India, almost all senior positions are manned by deputationists from all over the country. However, the elected representatives of the Corporation, instead of purging any discrimination against the officers on deputation, always proved to be masters of wordplay and double entendre. In other words, they would divide the officers on deputation and pit them against each other. So instead of working sincerely, the officers would be busy in settling scores with each other.

There are about thirty-nine departments in the Corporation. The Recruitment Rules framed for the personnel, particularly in the regulatory departments, do not provide for promotion to senior positions in the

Corporation, except for the labour department. It is but natural that whatever senior positions to which local officials are posted come from the labour department, which I discovered later was a kind of ruse played by some officials in the distant past to get the Recruitment Rules framed in this manner, thus depriving all other cadres of promotions to senior positions in the Corporation. Generally, local officers feel threatened when officers come on deputation, as they think their chances of promotion may be affected in some way.

OFFICERS MAKETH THE ORGANIZATION

There was an officer on deputation to the Corporation from the Central Government. He was straightforward, honest, effective, result-oriented and practical in the sense that he knew how to work with all the stakeholders as a team. However, many of the councillors over a period of time developed a strong dislike for this officer. This example is being quoted to bring home the point that any organization mandated to serve the public needs officers who are true to themselves. The procedure for extension of the period on deputation requires approval of the House of the Corporation. The proposal put up before the House in the form of a Preamble (as required under the relevant rules) was turned down on several occasions. I had to take the approval of the administrator of the Corporation on each occasion. The administrator (i.e. the LG of Delhi) has the delegated powers provided in the Delhi Municipal Corporation Act, 1957 to give the direction that a particular Resolution shall not be implemented. The councillors obviously were not interested in furthering the good work being done by the officer even as they all got united in favour of another deputationist, who had to be sent back at the earliest.

I can recall a number of instances where I had to make special efforts to retain work-oriented and honest officers in the Corporation, as many were opposed to their continuance in office. These officers had the courage to call a spade a spade. They also had the ability to lead from the front by example. As it happens, such officers, disliked for their honesty and zeal to work hard in delivering effective civic services, are not wanted when they are stumbling blocks in others' agenda. The tenures of such officers—unless there is a strong and imminent ground for shifting them out—are required to be fixed through administrative instructions to protect public interest.

There were exceptions as well. There was one particular case in which the entire Deliberative Wing got united in favour of a deputationist who used to masquerade as a panjandrum to reportedly harass all the officers.

There was also total unity among the councillors in the case of an official who served the Corporation on deputation from the Government of India by misrepresenting his designation (stating that he was of a particular rank, which he was not). He committed an illegal act, leading to registration of a case on various other charges. The CBI approached me for grant of prosecution sanction against the official. It was, however, contended by the head of the personnel department of the Corporation that since the official had reverted to his parent department, the prosecution sanction could only be given by the parent department, which was a ministry of the Government of India. The ministry concerned, however, redirected the matter with the comment that the misconduct related to a period when the official was on deputation to the MCD, and therefore, the appropriate prosecution-sanctioning authority would be the commissioner of the Corporation.

The environment in the Corporation seemed fully surcharged as the councillors were trying all possible means to save the official and all kinds of pressures were brought to bear on me. Resolutions were adopted by the committees and the House of the Corporation against the prosecution sanction granted by me. The main ground taken by the members of the Deliberative Wing was that I was not the prosecution-sanctioning authority, as the rules had not been amended in sync with the amendment made in 1993 in the Delhi Municipal Corporation Act, 1957.

Prior to 1993, the House of the Corporation was the prosecution-sanctioning authority for officers of the level of those on deputation. The legal position is that once an amendment is made in the parent Act, it takes precedence, irrespective of any amendment in the rules. The opinion of the then solicitor general of India confirmed the above position. The then mayor, however, sought legal opinion from the attorney general of India, who opined that 'since the relevant Rule had not been amended, the House remained the prosecution-sanctioning authority notwithstanding amendment in the parent Act.' The then mayor wrote to the Union Home Secretary enclosing a copy of the legal opinion of the attorney general of India, requesting him to initiate departmental proceedings against the commissioner who had overstepped his authority. The Union Home Secretary wrote to the Government of Delhi to take appropriate action in the matter based on the legal opinion of the attorney general. The then LG took up the matter with the Union Home Secretary, asserting that a provision in the Act would always take precedence. The behaviour of many of the councillors underwent a change overnight and they did not spare any chance to inveigh against me, such was the influence of the official. The matter reached the court of law and the judgement of the High Court was in accordance with the opinion of the attorney general of India. I did not follow the matter any further.

The official concerned had the temerity to write to me stating that I had ruined his life, in a way threatening me. This was done at the behest of the members of the

Deliberative Wing, who then approached me with a request to take back the officer on deputation and post him as the secretary to the commissioner. Such mutually beneficial liaisons can by no means be a positive sign for the organization. It is a kind of a symbiotic relationship using the scarce resources of the local body for their self-interest without any benefit to the general public.

THE REVENUE CONUNDRUM

It is sad that those who talk of making the organization self-reliant do very little to expand the revenue-earning base due to conflict of interests, and also tacitly allow the poachers to continue their illegal activities. It is common knowledge that the local body requires funds for various projects to provide and maintain basic services to the citizens. This could be done efficiently and on time if the Corporation generated enough revenue to augment its income, which should ideally be more than the expenditure. The revenues, instead of rightfully coming into the coffers of the Corporation, go to the wheeler-dealers.

The commissioner is required to prepare and present the budget annually. A number of proposals relating to the expansion of the revenue-earning base or augmentation of revenues of the Corporation, prepared year after year, were summarily rejected and negated the very next day. This was done by calling a special meeting of the Standing Committee, as the proposals did not 'suit' the election manifesto of the party in power. Such actions of the Deliberative Wing were totally iniquitous, as the proposals were not even discussed—proposals which would otherwise make the organization financially, functionally and ethically strong. They were simply dismissed. If such a situation continues, it will be well-nigh impossible to implement many of the reforms vital for ensuring basic living conditions to the citizens.

The financial health of the local body should be improved to create a corpus of funds. These funds and the accruing interest on such deposits should be used to pay the wages and salaries of the employees on time. This in turn will keep them motivated to work in the best interests of the organization and the public. The corpus of funds could be created by slowly eliminating wasteful expenditure and by widening the tax base through a robust system of tax collection, among others.

Political parties also need to see beyond their narrowed sense of self-righteousness to allow for the widening of revenue-collecting base and release of funds at the beginning of the financial year. We have had enough of political correctness. It is now time to demonstrate to the general public or the common man that efficiency of public services and utilities can improve only by making investments and that the money for such investments can come only by levying taxes or charges on the citizens.

The allocation of funds should not be left to the discretion of any particular committee or individual. It should be decided based on the merit of each case and the decision should be taken by a neutral body. The guiding principle should be the larger public good and certainly not the whims and fancies of any one person. It is because of such attitudes and behaviour that only a few officers are unafraid of taking bold decisions. It takes courage to stymie inappropriate proposals with negative revenue impact; for example, in the case of the domestic breeding checkers.

After the outbreak of dengue, sometime in 1996–97, it was decided to enlist around 2,500 workers to be designated as domestic breeding checkers. Many precious lives had been lost due to dengue fever and even after 1996, positive cases of dengue were regularly reported every year. The domestic breeding checkers were seasonal workers engaged for six months every year—from 1 May to 31 October. There were demands from these workers to regularize their services, which was not possible as per the extant rules and did not make any sense, as they were seasonal workers. They were, however, determined to get their temporary employment regularized.

Meanwhile, the need to collect property tax from all the households in the city was also under active consideration in the Corporation, as only around 15 lakh households paid property tax against 45 lakh households in the city (during 2010–11). Therefore, to bring the remaining households under the property tax net, it was proposed to use the services of the domestic breeding checkers from 1 November to 30 April. The proposal was approved by the Corporation, as it would augment the revenue earnings of the Corporation. The workers, however, wanted their services to be regularized without working as property tax surveyors. They succeeded in getting a Resolution passed by the House of the Corporation in this regard. I was then required to implement the proposal, being the Chief Executive Officer (CEO) of the Corporation. However, since the Resolution was against the rules notified by the Government of India for the regularization of the services of temporary or contractual employees, it was not possible to implement it.

The administrator of the union territory of Delhi, who is also the administrator of the MCD, has the inherent powers under the governing act to give directions as per the delegated powers of the Central Government, and accordingly it was decided not to implement the Resolution.

The matter reached the High Court of Delhi on the ground that the commissioner of the Corporation, who was duty-bound to implement the Resolution, was not doing so. Therefore, he was required to be directed by the court to implement the Resolution. I was asked to appear in the court and to explain the position. When the court was informed that it was not appropriate to burden the Corporation with a liability of ₹22 crore when the workers were engaged only for six months, it found merit in the submission made by me. Therefore, the court did not give any direction for implementing the Resolution passed by the House of the Corporation.

UPHOLDING THE RULE OF LAW

All functionaries in the government and local bodies are required to work with due diligence to uphold the Rule of Law. Approval from the MCD was sought by a public sector construction company for a building that was to be used as a government office. The public sector company National Buildings Construction Corporation Ltd (NBCC), under the Ministry of Urban Development, applied for MCD approval for a building constructed for the income tax department. The MCD officers did not consider the request, as the deficiencies in the building clearly established the impunity with which the construction was done, which defied both the letter and the spirit of the building bye-laws. The income tax department—the client department—was compelled to shift into the building at the earliest, having invested huge funds in it. The officers of the public sector company, perhaps assuming that the officers of the Corporation would give the requisite permission under duress, advised the income tax department to fix a date for the inauguration of the building by the union finance minister. The information of the date of inauguration was sent to the MCD officers with a view to getting the permission expedited. However, the officers were not ready to approve the construction and give a certificate to that effect. The matter finally landed on my table. Although initially annoyed about the withholding of permission, I upheld my officers' explanation that the construction and design of the building did not conform to the provisions laid down in the building bye-laws, and therefore, it was not possible to give a completion certificate for the same. The matter was reported to the higher echelons in the Ministry of Finance. The revenue secretary spoke to me on the phone and expressed his displeasure regarding the completion certificate, which had not been issued even as the building was slated to be inaugurated by the finance minister in the following couple of days. I explained the deficiencies in the building and advised the revenue secretary to call off the inaugural programme of the building, which would save the government some possible embarrassment.

The revenue secretary was obviously annoyed and did not respond to my suggestion of calling off the inaugural ceremony. As we did not hear about it any further in the Corporation, it was presumed that the suggestion put to the revenue secretary had been accepted. The additional secretary in the Ministry of Finance who was looking after the department of direct taxes visited me. He seemed quite upset. He conveyed the displeasure of the government at the way the matter had been handled, and while departing, issued an open threat that he would have the MCD turned upside down on this account. He felt the Corporation had overstepped its jurisdiction and applied the rules or bye-laws by not reading them in practical terms—meaning thereby that the deficiencies, if any, could have been overlooked. Soon after, a meeting was called by the urban development secretary at the behest of the revenue secretary. The facts of the case and the applicable bye-laws were discussed. The construction agency had gone ahead with the construction of the building thinking that a government building would not be subjected to any scrutiny for compliance with the provisions of the relevant bye-laws. The agency refused to make the required changes to conform to the provisions of the bye-laws. A series of meetings were held, but the Corporation stuck to its stand. In case the officers of the Corporation had shown any complicity in the matter, private builders would prompt media persons to quiz the minister about the illegality of the construction and embarrass the government. The construction agency of the government should have been careful in ensuring compliance of the provisions of the bye-laws, instead of taking it for granted that a government building would, in any case, pass the test of scrutiny. The loss to the exchequer in such cases is incalculable and the building may not be safe and habitable.

The officers of the MCD were complimented for their stand and for upholding the Rule of Law. In the end, fair play is always rewarded.

THREE

CRACKING THE WHIP: TACKLING CIVIC ISSUES

The capital city of Delhi has three local bodies, namely the MCD (now divided into three bodies—North Delhi Municipal Corporation, South Delhi Municipal Corporation and East Delhi Municipal Corporation), the NDMC and the DCB. These local bodies look after civic services in their respective areas. Their areas of operation are well demarcated. The MCD, as one of the local government bodies, has the largest jurisdiction over the city of Delhi for the provision of civic amenities, and services, from water to roads, transport, drainage and sanitation. The MCD looks after 94 per cent of the total area of the city and the remaining 6 per cent is looked after by the NDMC

(3 per cent) and the DCB (3 per cent).[1] The MCD is the main local body, as it caters to 97 per cent of the total population residing in the city.

No doubt, the management of civic amenities in the areas under the control of the MCD is a challenging task; yet, that is only the tip of the iceberg. There is the problem of large-scale absenteeism on a daily basis, particularly of the safai karamcharis. This issue was comprehensively addressed by introducing the biometric system of marking attendance. The newly introduced system of marking attendance made a perceptible difference, as the supervisory officers, who also used to be relaxed, became alert and active. The physical presence of safai karamcharis and the supervisory officers helped the overall sanitation in the city.

Another significant aspect is the nature of built forms (i.e. constructed structures or buildings) under the jurisdiction of these bodies. Whereas there may only be a sprinkling of unauthorized or unplanned constructions in the areas under the jurisdiction of the NDMC and the DCB, the areas under the jurisdiction of the MCD are predominantly unauthorized and unplanned as a result of free-for-all development.

MANAGEMENT OF SANITATION INFRASTRUCTURE

Commercial and residential wastes generated in a municipal

[1]Ritam Haldar, 'Rule-breakers Treat Delhi as Garbage Bin', *Hindustan Times*, 2 December 2015

area in either solid or semi-solid form, excluding industrial hazardous wastes, constitute MSW. The Department of Environment Management Service (DEMS) of the MCD, which looks after the management of MSW, was mismanaged. The department is equipped with suitable infrastructure for waste management, including heavy vehicles, workshops for the repair of such vehicles, and stores for keeping the equipment and tools. However, the workshops for the repair of the garbage-clearing vehicles had become storehouses of old, redundant and unusable vehicles. When I visited the workshops, I found them enveloped in chaos.

Naturally, the efficiency of the department responsible for clearing garbage from all over the city is dependent on the management of repair operations of the garbage-clearing vehicles, duration of their repair time, availability of spare parts and the workforce responsible for repairs, among others. The availability of space in the workshops is also a crucial factor for upscaling the efficiency of garbage-clearing operations. There was no system for management of inventory of the various spare parts required for the repairing of the vehicles. There was no point in seeking clarification for the slow speed of clearing operations or delays in overall output. It was first necessary to clear the workshops of the clutter that had collected for years and was occupying precious space. A survey of the redundant vehicles and equipment was done with the help of a committee, which was also made responsible for fixing the reserve price for condemned vehicles and unusable store items. Following the auction and removal of the old vehicles, three-fourth of the space in the workshops was cleared.

A standard operating procedure (SOP) was needed to be put in place, as it would lay down the maximum time allowed for various kinds of repairs and also help optimize the cost of repairs through appropriate inventory management. The objective essentially was to facilitate the availability of more and more vehicles in good working condition to be used for garbage-clearing operations.

However, the exercise to draft the SOP took longer than required. The reasons were not hard to find. The prevalent system suited the staff, as the breakdown of more vehicles made it possible for them to sit idle. The formalities for making a purchase required time, as a procedure had to be followed, and therefore, in some cases, the repairs were unnecessarily delayed. This adversely affected the garbage-clearing operations.

After visiting the workshops, I could easily conclude that many of the personnel working there had not been properly trained in the repair of vehicles and equipment. In fact, many of them had picked up the technique simply by observing others. Repair work by such personnel only added to the cost of repair. It is unfortunate that no attention had ever been paid to systematically upgrade the workshops and to prescribe a SOP for them. The working of the grass-roots level of the machinery and workforce needs to be made foolproof, with a single-point authority for each discipline responsible for overseeing the operations. This would ensure completion of the assigned tasks efficiently and on time. The mandate of time-bound performance of the assigned tasks would make it possible to keep the city clean throughout and with regularity. The process of purchase of items required for sweeping the streets and roads also needs improvement to ensure quality and economy in public spending.

FIXING DELHI'S ROADS

The network of roads in the capital measures about 33,260 km (lane length). The PWD of the Government of Delhi looks after a length of around 1,200 km; the three MCDs take care of 23,931 km; the NDMC, the DCB and the National Highway Authority of India (NHAI) look after a length of 8,129 km. The maintenance of roads leaves much to be desired. The materials used in the construction of roads are required to be of good quality to ensure that they are maintenance-free. There may be a requirement to relay the roads after six or seven years of construction. However, what happens on the ground is altogether different, notwithstanding the 'Quality Control Laboratories' set up in the Corporation to check the quality of materials used for construction of buildings and roads. The examination of quality in the Quality Laboratory is done by sending samples of material with proven quality. The samples, therefore, would never fail. The cost of setting up the Quality Control Laboratory and the expenditure incurred for running it, is a kind of 'double jeopardy' for the Corporation, as the objective of ensuring quality is compromised case after case anyway. And to show impartiality in the examination of samples, a few of them are randomly declared 'unqualified'. All this is eyewash, as the samples of projects which involve substantial funds never seem to fail.

The root cause of the poor quality of roads, however, is related primarily to the system of lifting the samples of the materials used in the construction of roads. For instance, the proposal of sending the samples of materials to independent, non-profit institutions like the Shriram Centre for Industrial Research was always opposed. Instead, there were suggestions to get the samples examined anywhere, but only if they were selected by a designated team. The requirement, therefore, was to remove all traces of opacity in the process of checking of the quality of materials. One of the ways to achieve this could be to form citizens' committees for each area to pick the samples in a transparent manner. The members of the citizens' committee would pick out samples of materials in the presence of officials. Such a change in the system of lifting samples of materials for testing in the laboratory would not only help provide good quality of roads, it would also save precious public funds.

As mentioned earlier, the use of poor-quality materials in road construction would inevitably result in the requirement of repairs. The repairs were carried out by heating up a mixture of aggregates—small pieces of stones with coal tar. The heating of the mix facilitated its bonding with the surface of the road, just like an adhesive. But this process also caused smoke and pollution. In the 1990s, the courts stopped this practice. The operations of mixing the aggregates and coal tar were shifted to the borders of the capital. However, the time involved in transporting the mix from the borders to the repair sites reduced the temperature of the mix, especially during the winter season, whereby the mix would not permanently stick to the surface of the road, leading to potholes. The formation of potholes on the roads after the slightest precipitation was but natural. As they say, there is no love lost between water and coal tar and yet, no solution has been found to keep the aggregates and coal tar bound together in the presence of water.

ROADS AND WATERLOGGING: A RECURRENT PROBLEM

Year after year, the roads get damaged due to waterlogging. The monsoon season throws traffic out of gear with severe waterlogging for days at a stretch, almost throughout the city. The problem arises and the blame game starts between the traffic police and the local body.

The primary cause of waterlogging is the inadequacy in the city's network of eighteen storm water drains or nallahs carrying water from all over the city into the Yamuna, which moves with full force after heavy rains.[2] However, the level of water in the Yamuna in the 22-km stretch through Delhi[3] also rises steadily as more and more water is released from the neighbouring state of Haryana, which regulates the release of water as and when required to save the adjoining villages in the upper reaches from getting inundated. As the water level in the river rises, storm water from the city cannot flow into the river. In fact, the water from the river enters the city through the nallahs and there is always a risk of some adjoining areas getting flooded as a result of the back flow of the river water.

With a view to preventing the river water from entering the city, sluice gates were installed at the mouths of the nallahs. After the sluice gates are closed, the storm water cannot be discharged into the Yamuna, and therefore, it collects on the roads and open grounds in the nearby areas. The duration of waterlogging in the areas ranges from a few hours to days, depending on the mood of Yamuna River in spate.

While the absence of adequate drainage in the capital city is not breaking news, any effort to improve the system by any singular department is striking against a wall for the simple reason that the city roads are owned and managed

---

[2]Sushmita Sengupta, 'What drains mean to cities', Down to Earth, 17 August 2015, accessed 1 July 2019, https://www.downtoearth.org.in/news/what-drains-mean-to-cities-44069

[3]http://www.yamunagentlyweeps.com/theyamuna.html, accessed 18 June 2019

by four or five agencies. In addition, there are also various agencies and authorities looking after public utilities who dig up the roads. The lack of interdepartmental coordination eventually leads to chaos year after year. The poor design of the road endings, turnings and crossroads; leakages in the trunk sewers and water line; the digging up of roads and the improper rebuilding of the dug-up structures, resulting in potholes, are also some additional reasons for the stagnant water on the roads. And this is only half of the real causes.

The regularity of cleaning operations involving the removal of silt from the nallahs and shifting it in the same form (without leaving it behind on the ground to dry up) would ensure that the roadsides are clean and there is no waterlogging. The implementation of the recommendation made in the master plan for the repair and relay of the network of drains prepared by the Indian Institute of Technology (IIT) Delhi would take some time for effective implementation.[4] Until then, extra efforts need to be made to take care of the critical points and stretches of the roads

---

[4]Abhishek Anand, 'IIT Delhi devises drainage masterplan to prevent waterlogging in the city', *India Today*, 3 August 2018, accessed 18 June 2019, https://www.indiatoday.in/india/story/iit-delhi-devises-drainage-masterplan-to-prevent-waterlogging-in-the-city-1304314-2018-08-03

BI India Bureau, 'IIT Delhi has a master drainage plan for the Capital, but it remains unimplemented', *Business Insider India*, 19 July 2018, accessed 18 June 2019, https://www.businessinsider.in/iit-delhi-has-a-master-drainage-plan-for-the-capital-but-it-remains-unimplemented/articleshow/65052551.cms

where waterlogging takes place year after year and which have already been identified.

The upkeep of the drain which is under the control of the local bodies needs to be assigned to the Delhi Sanitation Task Force (DSTF)—an agency proposed to be set up on the lines of the Delhi Metro Rail Corporation Ltd. It would look after the collection of the MSW from the households and deposit them in the underground containers located in the vicinity of each colony or residential area, transportation of the MSW to the processing sites, management of the processing sites, the scientific disposal of sewage (at present under the DJB), and the setting up and maintenance of public toilets or washrooms and the drains all over the city.

There are also other solutions to prevent road damage caused by waterlogging. Water harvesting in such areas is required to facilitate its absorption in the substratum for storage. The roads adjoining the eighteen nallahs need to be specially designed and converted to RCC roads. The funds needed for the road infrastructure could be substantially reduced by properly maintaining them. This is also one way to cut down wasteful expenditure. Each sector needs to be provided an SOP to save funds. The savings thus made could be put to good use in discharging the obligatory as well as discretionary functions without having to depend on grants from the Government of Delhi/India.

COLLAPSING PUBLIC HEALTH INFRASTRUCTURE

The management of public health is a key area requiring major investment. The MCD provides healthcare facilities through six major hospitals and a large number of dispensaries spread over the entire area of its jurisdiction.

A visit to the Hindu Rao Hospital, one of the largest government hospitals in Delhi, would reveal a state of utter chaos due to the ever-increasing number of patients both in the outpatient department (OPD) as well as those who need admission for treatment. The infrastructure available therefore needs to be urgently upgraded.

The space in Hindu Rao Hospital, located on the hilly terrain of the Aravalli Hills, is highly constrained due to the very nature of its setting. Vehicles are parked all over the place, leaving very little space for the pedestrians. It is imperative to add on to the built-up space to maintain basic standards. Additionally, there is the need to reconstruct almost all the buildings which seem to have been impulsively constructed—almost as an afterthought. The conditions of the other hospitals of the Corporation are also not very encouraging. The building infrastructure of the all the hospitals is required to be upgraded and augmented to meet the growing requirements in a time-bound manner. This is necessary to improve the services being provided in the outpatient departments as well as the services in the wards for the patients admitted in the hospitals.

The idea to set up a Medical College under the

Corporation had been under consideration for quite some time. It however could not fructify due to constrains imposed by the non-availability of funds to engage a consultant, among other factors. In-house planning for such an important venture was considered risky for various reasons. Meanwhile, a spirited and highly motivated officer who had worked in the All India Institute of Medical Sciences (AIIMS) joined the Corporation. He volunteered to work on the project, and eventually, the proposal was approved by the Corporation. The facilities for setting up a Medical College attached to the Hindu Rao Hospital therefore needed to be planned with a perspective to ensure smooth growth of the institution thereafter and for all times to come. The unique aspect of setting up the Medical College related to the in-house planning and execution done by the officers of the Corporation, which made for a case study to be taught in Management schools.

The planning of an institution of this magnitude was not an easy task, even more so in a political milieu where any wrong move in planning or execution could manifest in unpleasant situations or mudslinging. The Hindu Rao Medical College is one of the most recent feathers in the glorious cap of the MCD.[5] It is a matter of satisfaction that the Medical College is growing into an institution of

[5]Baishali Adak, 'Delhi: Hindu Rao Hospital will soon get a facelift by North MCD', *India Today*, 26 December 2017, accessed 18 June 2019, https://www.indiatoday.in/mail-today/story/delhi-hindu-rao-hospital-facelift-north-mcd-1116152-2017-12-26

academic excellence, thanks to the untiring efforts of all those who conceived the idea and made it see the light of day.

There is similarly a pressing need to utilize the surplus land available in the precincts of the RBTB Hospital at Kingsway Camp in North Delhi. The surplus land in the hospital could be commercially exploited to build up a corpus of reserve funds. This can be started with a meagre amount, which can then gradually grow to reach an amount sufficient enough to fetch interest. This interest amount can be further used to pay the wages and salaries of the staff. The surplus land could be developed into commercial properties, just like the projects developed by the NDMC. The NDMC—a small local body with an area less than a ward of the MCD—is almost independent, as the revenue earned from its commercial ventures, such as hotels, office spaces, etc. is enough to take care of the funds required for various activities, including its salary bills. The proposal of creating a corpus of reserve funds may sound like a temporary measure to those who may have been observing the functioning of the local body from the sidelines. This, however, is a permanent solution. The only condition is that none other than the Central Government should have the power to allow withdrawal of money from the corpus. The accruing interest should however be used by the local body for paying the salaries of the workers and employees. Any wasteful expenditure being incurred on non-essential activities or on projects where there is no guarantee of the assets being sustained for a reasonably long period needs to be curtailed and efficiently managed.

HOSPITAL (MIS)MANAGEMENT

The management of healthcare services is highly specialized and it is necessary to ensure availability of the requisite infrastructure—medicines, equipment, staff—and its close supervision to sustain efficient health services in a hospital. Given that services available in private hospitals are expensive and beyond the reach of the common man, it is important that similar services in the government-run hospitals are made available without the heavy burden of costs of medicines, procedures and examinations or tests. The management of these services in public hospitals would, therefore, require optimal utilization of space, services, medicines and time.

I needed to periodically visit the hospitals run by the MCD to instil a sense of discipline among the staff. There were some doctors who were engaged in private practice, in violation of the extant rules which forbid such practice and compensate the doctors by paying them Non Practising Allowance (NPA). These doctors had got themselves assigned administrative duties and still had the audacity to be involved in private practice. All sincere efforts to further streamline the delivery of healthcare services in the hospitals are marred by this could-not-care-less attitude.

The procurement of medicines and hospital equipment is another grey area which needs to be made more transparent. It would help if the MCD consulted the Delhi government or the Central Government in making estimates of the annual requirements of medicines and healthcare equipment. This work can be assigned to a committee of experts comprising members of the accounts, finance and health departments, who would make the purchases in a centralized manner at least six months in advance. The supplies to the hospitals or dispensaries would be made on the basis of indents signed by the medical superintendents of the hospital concerned along with a certified copy of the utilization certificate to be signed by the departmental head of each speciality. The equipment also should be upgraded to keep pace with the latest technologies. This would help public hospitals provide treatments at par with the private hospitals.

The local body also developed an Integrated Disease Surveillance Programme (IDSP) for timely reporting of communicable diseases such as cholera, dengue, malaria, etc. Login IDs and passwords were given to all the hospitals for online reporting. This facilitated the taking of timely action in preventing the spread of such diseases. Likewise, online registration of births and deaths was simplified.

QUALITY OF EDUCATION

The progress of a nation is linked to the system and practice of imparting education, particularly in the primary schools; i.e. in the formative years of a child. If there is just one area that requires undivided attention of the planners, educationists and administrators for making the burgeoning population economically independent, it is the system of teaching in schools, which at present leaves much to be desired. The emphasis thus far is on providing midday meals, text books and uniforms or jerseys. The objective of the policymakers is to motivate parents of children of the economically backward sections of society to send their wards to schools. The entire year, however, passes without receiving the uniforms and other essential supplies, mainly due to the general apathy of officials. Delay in receipt of supplies adds to the problem, as learning cannot be squeezed out of textbooks received by the end of the term and a jersey cannot be worn during the summer months.

Another serious concern is the quality of education being imparted in the schools. The entire machinery of the department of education in the local body remains busy the whole year round in making purchases of text books, jerseys, midday meals, furniture and other miscellaneous items. There is hardly any effort in improving the quality of education. The teachers play a mechanical role, as there is no connect between the teachers and the taught. When teachers are unable to make learning interesting, it only distracts the students. The social background of the children who attend the schools of the municipalities does not provide any support for learning. For the families of these children, school is a waste of time, as they would rather be busy in earning money to sustain their existence. The supply of midday meals in schools is an attraction for the families, as they consider it a way of supplementing the food requirement of their children (some of them are not even entitled to have a square meal a day). There is no time for these children to sit and study at home, as they are kept busy with odd jobs by the parents. Their education is certainly not on the parents' priority list. Therefore, the time available in the school needs to be fully utilized to enable them to learn. Teachers, therefore, need to be mandated to inculcate good learning habits in the school students.

It is proven beyond doubt that the inequalities between the lower and upper strata of society could be bridged by improving the quality of education in the schools run by government or municipalities. However, if the teachers are generally absent from schools or busy politicking or doing jobs of an administrative nature, the students suffer. Almost all the teachers in all the schools act like janitors—as if they have been engaged to lock and unlock the herds of young children in classrooms at fixed hours. Their duty does not seem to involve inspiring learning in children. Hence, the performance appraisal of teachers must be done in a manner that helps to eliminate the deadwood amongst them.

Before joining as the commissioner (MCD) in 2008, I was the additional commissioner (MCD) in charge of Education and Health from 1999–2001. I also served in the education department of the Government of Delhi in 1986 for about a year. Hence, I have had first-hand experience of the workings of schools in the MCD as well as the Delhi government.

It is a known fact that the premises of the schools are not often kept neat and clean. It is quite common to find all kinds of waste lying on the ground almost everywhere. There are also instances of open defecation taking place in the schools, just behind the walls of the classrooms adjoining the boundary walls. I discovered to my horror that the principal and the teachers pretended to be unaware of the faeces lying in the premises of the schools. The environment in the schools is therefore far from being conducive to good learning. Further, there are no separate washrooms for the girls who choose not to use the ones in the school for as long as they are there.

The prevailing conditions in the schools can be gauged from this simple example. Once, the principal of a school on being asked to drink the water that she proudly claimed to be potable, refused to do so. During one of my inspection rounds of schools, I peeped into the pitcher of water kept there and found it to be infested with insects, sand and other kinds of filth. Even as there is no dearth of resources provided by the government or local body, those who should motivate and cultivate interest of learning in the students just refuse to do their duties sincerely.

The system of supervision is very poor and lax. It is difficult to evaluate the performance of teachers, as there are no examinations at the end of the academic session. And with almost everyone passing in the examinations till a certain level or grade, there is no system to measure the learning achieved by a child. The future of these children appears bleak, as eventually they will either drop out or get initiated into the world of crime. The teachers are more interested in getting their salaries. The political patronage gives the teachers a kind of shield from any action taken by sincere supervisory officers. The teachers' associations and unions also come in the way of any disciplinarian approach adopted by the administration. The final outcome therefore is to allow the status quo—a system of mechanical learning with no checks and balances. The future of the students is not safe unless the system of performance appraisal of the teachers is made foolproof.

The number of students attending the municipal schools and the ones run by the Delhi government has been steadily decreasing over the years. There are informal reports of overstating the enrolment, as the teachers have a vested interest in preventing the school from being merged with another one or closed, or the strength of teachers in a particular school being reduced to avoid wasteful expenditure. The parents withdraw their wards from schools run by the local body or government, as there is a perceived lack of interest from the school authorities in making learning a pleasurable experience. The amount of time spent in these schools is considered as a waste, as the children are not able to read or write, let alone solve mathematical sums or understand other intricate matters of life and the prospective careers they may like to pursue. The need of the hour is to recruit teachers who are motivated as well as knowledgeable in the methods of initiating young children into the process of learning and can do so in a playful manner. All this requires an innate quality of getting thoroughly involved in the tasks required or assigned. The upkeep of the premises of the schools, supported with the basic infrastructure and a foolproof mechanism of supplying uniforms, textbooks, jerseys and midday meals is a prerequisite. It would therefore be needed to create an infrastructure to procure and distribute these items independently in coordination with the head of the school.

Another important area that is central to improving the quality of education relates to the training of the teachers—both at the time of recruitment as well as in-service training. This will help improve and sharpen the skills of teaching the tiny tots—a very challenging task that is taken so lightly, even by the policymakers. An educated nation is a strong nation. The self-assured policymakers need to be woken up to the ground realities before it is too late!

ROOF FOR THE ROOFLESS

Homelessness is a civic issue everywhere in the country, particularly in the capital. While India had a recorded number of 13 million homeless people, there were 56,000 homeless in Delhi in 2010.[6] Thousands of people come to Delhi in search of employment. It may well be easier to find some employment in the city than shelter for the night. Even rented 'shanties' (thatched huts) are expensive for those with meagre earnings. Multitudes of homeless and hapless residents of the city are compelled to occupy public spaces and live there temporarily and then permanently. As a matter of principle and under the legal framework, no one is authorized to squat on any public space. What however happens is just the contrary. Sleeping on pavements is illegal, but the illegality, however, cannot outweigh the requirement of human existence. For these squatters, the summer months are easier to bear than the winters, when it is not possible to sleep in the open anywhere in the freezing cold.

The state makes arrangements by setting up temporary as well as permanent night shelters with separate segments for men and women. There is however always a shortage of space, as the requirement keeps on fluctuating depending on weather conditions. The state provides facilities in the night

[6] Geeta Gupta, '56,000 homeless in Delhi, finds UNDP', *The Indian Express*, 8 December 2011, accessed 18 June 2019, https://indianexpress.com/article/cities/delhi/56-000-homeless-in-delhi-finds-undp/

shelters such as drinking water, water coolers, beds, durries, blankets, first-aid boxes, fire extinguishers, etc. There are separate arrangements for children, families, differently abled persons and women.

The removal of encroachers at a time of the year when it is cold does not go down well with anyone, even if they are outrightly illegal settlements. I remember one such case in which the local-level functionary removed a few families from the parks located on the main road during the last week of December. There was a public furore and a public interest litigation (PIL) was filed in the High Court of Delhi. The court was not pleased with the timing of the encroachment-removal action, which was indeed ill-timed, and therefore, directions were issued to restore the settlements for the duration of the winter.

What could be a foolproof solution to ensure shelter for all? No one should become a victim of the vagaries of the weather. The capital city of Delhi is characterized by extreme weather—people die of extreme cold and from heat strokes. It should therefore be ensured that there are facilities for such persons to stay till they are able to make alternative arrangements. It would however be important to clearly establish the identity of the person needing shelter—the proof of identity should be the Aadhaar Card. In case Aadhaar Card is not available, arrangements need to be made to get the details of the person verified through the state government. This will ensure that scarce resources of the state are saved and that antisocial elements are not able to exploit the system.

The practice of setting up night shelters anywhere and everywhere needs to be changed, as ultimately it leads to unpleasant situations of all kinds, from traffic-related issues to unhygienic conditions. It would be prudent to set apart some space in all the areas for this. The construction of a suitable building would avoid the recurrent expenditure of setting up temporary shelters. A multipurpose building would however need to be well secured with a high-level boundary wall and with CCTVs installed at critical points to keep a constant vigil on the happenings inside the building. The complex of a night shelter should have all facilities needed to make the stay of the occupants comfortable, such as washrooms, kitchens, and laundry facilities, among others. The duration of stay of each inmate would be monitored to prevent them from making night shelters their permanent abodes, and to give everyone a fair share of the benefit. The CEO of the Delhi Urban Shelter Improvement Board (DUSIB) should be made responsible for ensuring the use of such shelters only for a bona fide purpose. It should be appreciated that such an arrangement would bring benefits to the society at large by controlling insanitation in and around areas where shelters are set up and keeping public health issues at bay, as when sanitation is properly maintained, there is almost no risk to the public health. And most of all, providing shelter to homeless persons protects them from all kinds of dangers, ranging from sexual assault to fatal harassment.

DEALING WITH DEATH

The cremation of dead bodies in the city of Delhi is being done in fifty-nine traditional cremation grounds spread around the city. There are also three CNG and one electricity-fuelled crematoriums that are seldom used, apart from around thirteen burial grounds in the city. It is the Corporation's responsibility to provide and maintain the infrastructure for seamless performance of the last rites and related activities in a subtle and solemn manner.

The Corporation took up a number of initiatives to streamline the various activities associated with cremation of dead bodies at the Nigambodh Ghat, one of the largest cremation grounds in the city. Projects related to expansion and creation of proper parking lots with controlled entry or exit gates and levelling the ground to facilitate the easy flow of water were needed. Construction and maintenance of prayer or meeting halls and the addition of pyres with proper shade and chimneys were inter alia implemented. It was, however, reported that even after providing the requisite infrastructure, the personnel deployed to oversee the activities were not sensitive to the solemnity of the occasion. There were reports that to make some extra money, the contractors were supplying wet wood in connivance with the officials of the local body looking after the ghat in the public health department of Civil Lines Zone. Cleanliness of the complex also requires attention, as the workload keeps on increasing. There are also requirements of a particular community to set up the pyre on the bank of the Yamuna close to the water. After the dead body burns to ashes, the remains are pushed into the river. The area all around therefore is required to be kept in good shape. As repeated instructions to the lower-level officials regarding this were falling on deaf ears, it was deemed necessary to involve dedicated volunteers to handle all the services at the ghat in a manner befitting the occasion.

A number of civil society groups and NGOs were keen to take over the operations without being paid more than a reasonable amount. The officials at the lower levels were, however, not ready to allow any outsiders to take over the operations, for obvious reasons. A syndicate of vicious contractors, officials and those performing the rite was working as a cohort to block any attempt to bring in operators from outside. The proposals submitted by the interested groups would be kept pending in the hope that they would soon be forgotten.

Things came to a pass when a particular group brought these misdeeds to my notice. I was at a loss initially. I could not understand why anyone working at the ghat would come in the way of such a proposal, that too from a philanthropic group. The group, on the other hand, was willing to invest funds for bettering the services at the ghat. I therefore decided to personally pursue the matter. The Deliberative Wing was satisfied with the proposal. The group finally succeeded in overcoming all the hurdles coming in their way for years. The shape of services underwent a sea change after the group took over the services. The ghat underwent a major facelift following that.

The performance of rituals at the time of cremation requires wood. A traditional human pyre takes around six hours and burns 400–500 kg of wood[7]. There are electric or CNG crematoria (which would be environmentally beneficial) set up in the city which have not become popular with the citizens, as almost everybody prefers to burn the dead body on the traditional pyre. This is however a very sensitive issue that needs to be addressed urgently. The general public must be made aware of the harmful effects of using wood for burning dead bodies. They should be encouraged to shift from the traditional system of cremation to alternative methods.

It has been estimated that funeral pyres in our country consume around fifty to sixty million trees a year[8] leading to generation of five lakh tonnes of ash and eight million tonnes of carbon dioxide. Adoption of alternative techniques

---

[7]Tanvi Patel, 'A Cremation Requires Some 500 kg of Wood; Here Are Some Green Alternatives', The Better India, 3 January 2018, accessed 18 June 2019, https://www.thebetterindia.com/126580/cremation-wood-green-alternatives/

[8]Ibid.

or methods of cremation could prevent felling of millions of trees every year and also bring down the pollution caused by the burning of wood. The initial reluctance of the general public to make the shift could be overcome slowly and steadily if the benefits are disseminated in the form of stories and by clarifying that there is no need to compromise on any ritual.

We also need to assuage the sentiments of the pet lovers in the city. As of now, there are no earmarked spaces for the burial of the dead bodies of the pets and the hapless owners are left to find such spaces in their neighbourhoods—if there are any available open spaces and if no one objects to it. It is without doubt that the feelings of grief and sorrow are no less at the passing away of a pet, comparable in equal measure to the loss of someone in the family. Adequate space should therefore be earmarked for performing the last rites of these faithful friends of the human race.

LITTERING: A MENACE

It is common knowledge that spitting in public places or littering of streets and roads is commonly done by residents in transit. Instead of carrying the waste back to their homes, they throw them all around the city. If all the residents carry the leftovers and garbage back to their homes or deposit them in the receptacles kept for that purpose, and if pet owners carry litter bags with them, the garbage can be contained and our city will be cleaner. Alongside educating the citizens, there is requirement of a provision in the law which could act as a deterrent against such practices.

Following the directives issued by the High Court of Delhi in a PIL case and as a follow-up action for preventing littering all around in the city, arrangements were made year after year by the Corporation to that effect. The overall impact of such arrangements, however, has not been encouraging. The deployment of special executive magistrates or municipal magistrates drawn from a cross section of disciplines did not make any difference, barring a few areas where those who were deployed walked the extra mile to not only enforce the relevant provisions in the letter and spirit of the law but also educate the public at large to bring about civic discipline.

Even political parties are not averse to their own share of littering. The most vulnerable period is a few months before an election poll when the number of posters, bills and pamphlets registers a sharp increase. Hoardings, posters and bills cover each nook and corner of the city even though the authorities managing the election process have prescribed norms for the campaigns. The impunity with which almost all political parties engage in such illegal acts is on full display.

All over the city, trees, pillars, electricity poles and the boundary walls of buildings facing the road are plastered with posters and pamphlets. When the glue dries up, or after a bout of rainfall, these posters fall off the walls and lie strewn across streets and pedestrian walkways. This not only adds to insanitation, but it is also illegal in as much as it encroaches upon public spaces. The governing act of the local body prescribes the use of such public spaces for the augmentation of the Corporation's revenues through the display of advertisements at certain locations not considered hazardous for drivers of vehicles.

Several citizens' groups have been active in helping the civic body to deal with the menace of posters. It is a matter of concern that despite them coming into force from 1 March 2009,[9] the provisions of the Delhi Prevention of Defacement of Property Act, 2007 are not being enforced. As per the provisions of the Act, 'sticking of posters, banners and wall writings on the properties in public view is an illegal act and is a cognisable offence.' The penalty under the Act is up to ₹50,000 or jail up to one year or both.[10]

However, lawbreakers continue to break the rules; they pay the fine and settle the cases but are back again to getting their message conveyed through all means possible, to win the political race.

Not only the walls of the city, but even its entire skyline

---

[9]http://www.delhipolice.nic.in/The%20Delhi%20Prevention%20of%20Defacement%20of%20Property%20Act.pdf, accessed 19 June 2019

[10]Staff Reporter, 'Delhi to observe Poster-Free Day,' *The Hindu*, 21 August 2009, accessed 19 June 2019, https://www.thehindu.com/news/cities/Delhi/Delhi-to-observe-Poster-Free-Day/article16876081.ece

is cluttered with the presence of 'discs' and a jumble of crisscrossing cables of telecom operators and carriers providing Internet services. The wires or cables for cable TV and Internet connections should be kept underground to maintain the aesthetics of the city landscape. The local bodies and police personnel need to work in close coordination to keep the city free of posters and overhanging cables.

With the revolution brought about by advancement in information and mobile technology, messages could easily be spread across society and target groups through a variety of communication channels, including the use of Internet, WhatsApp, emails and social media—all without defacing the city. There is no barrier of language and the messages could easily be transcribed or translated as well and made available to anyone and everywhere. If there are still issues relevant to only a few and in select areas beset with the problem of digital divide, billboards could be erected where messages could be pasted freely and easily. The better informed, and those in quest of information, could be reached by sending posters, ads, etc. through newspapers. The regulation of all these activities would bring order on the roads and also augment the revenue collection of the local body.

FOUR

UNCOMMON CHALLENGES OF THE COMMONWEALTH GAMES

The hosting of the Commonwealth Games 2010 in Delhi provided an opportunity to further improve and strengthen the civic infrastructure of the city. As the preparation for the Games started much before the actual Games, it was possible to prepare plans and execute them in an appropriate manner. There was a frenzy of activities in the run-up to the Games. Everyone in the government seemed busy in the preparations. Amidst frantic efforts to meet the targets, review meetings were held by a dozen authorities, stoking the officers in charge to complete the assigned work before the deadlines. The city spruced up and it wore a new look. The unique sense of discipline and the general conduct of the common citizens were exemplary; a self-imposed charter of dos and don'ts descended on everyone's mindset. The efforts of officers across departments were praiseworthy, considering the constraints of time and the condescending attitudes of some of the authorities in charge of holding the Games, even as they worked in trepidation throughout. A number of bold initiatives were taken by the MCD.

FIXING ENCROACHMENTS

The Ministry of Tourism provided financial assistance for showcasing the country's heritage and for improving the surroundings of the guest houses located particularly in Karol Bagh and Paharganj,[11] these being important commercial centres and closer to the New Delhi Railway Station (commonly known as NDLS). The work to improve the surroundings of the guest houses and facilitate access to them included the widening of roads through the removal of the encroachments, among other things. The tangle of electricity and telephone cables was to be taken under the ground. All these required close coordination with the respective departments, including those dealing with public utilities—a tall order indeed.

[11]Ruhi Bhasin, 'Paharganj set to get makeover', *The Times of India*, 9 June 2010, accessed 19 June 2019, https://timesofindia.indiatimes.com/city/delhi/Paharganj-set-to-get-makeover/articleshow/6025951.cms

The roadsides in these areas had been encroached upon by local dhabas, cycle and car repair shops, and apothecaries and hakims for many years, and many of them even claimed ownership. A balanced approach however was adopted to remove the encroachments—by firmly telling them that they had no right to squat on public land, and certainly could not violate the right of way. Such an approach had a prophylactic effect, as any undue haste would have provoked the lawbreakers to arraign the officials concerned on false criminal charges. The success of all the encroachment-removal campaigns of the MCD in Paharganj is a testimony to the perseverance, tactfulness and deft handling of the situation by the then DC of the Paharganj zone of the Corporation.

A bigger challenge was removing the encroachments in front of Shiela Cinema. The vehicles—cycle rickshaws, buses, cars and hand carts—moving in both directions were forced to use the road in front of the cinema, as there was no road on the other side connecting the New Delhi Railway Station with Paharganj. It had not been possible to build a one-way road on the side of the Amrit Kaur Market leading from the New Delhi Railway Station to Paharganj. The electricity transformer close to the Amrit Kaur Market was coming in the way. Also, there were a number of unauthorized small shops around the transformer and they had the audacity to prevaricate when asked to remove the encroachments from the public land. However, wise counsel prevailed and they realized the futility of their stand and removed the unauthorized portions voluntarily. The unauthorized extensions in front of the shops on the main road leading to Connaught Place were also removed, and the choked drains were redesigned. The removal of the illegal encroachments and the shifting of the transformer paved the way for the building of a road connecting the New Delhi Railway Station to the main bazaar of Paharganj.

The one-way movement of traffic eased the heavy congestion in the stretch from the Paharganj Police Station to the New Delhi Railway Station, much to the relief of the commuters, who sometimes had to wait for hours to reach the railway station from the Paharganj side. The confusion caused by vehicles moving in the wrong direction was removed by erecting a concrete road divider of a sufficient height, which ensured that all the vehicles moved on the authorized right of way only. All these initiatives reduced the travel time from Paharganj to the New Delhi Railway Station.

PUBLIC CONVENIENCES

The surging crowds in front of the New Delhi Railway Station need public conveniences. To handle the volume of discharge, washrooms and toilets of appropriate capacity were constructed. The entire area of Paharganj and Karol Bagh was given a facelift and there was a perceptible change in the ambience of the surroundings of the guest houses there, with the hanging wires shifted underground.

The public conveniences need to be improved regularly every year, keeping in mind the growth of population in the city. The Corporation introduced three new types of public conveniences. Two waterless toilets were set up at Town Hall and Kashmere Gate Inter State Bus Terminus (ISBT); the two sites with the heaviest footfall. The technology ensured that there was no foul smell and no need of using water. The technology used was, however, not found to be cost effective. Toilets developed by the Defence Research and Development Organisation (DRDO) of the Ministry of Defence were set up at Nigambodh Ghat.[12] These toilets had been designed and developed for the army personnel posted at Siachen. The claim of the DRDO was confirmed, as the toilets were efficient and useful. There was, however, some difficulty in placing orders with the agency finalized by the DRDO due to some technical and procedural constraints.

A company based in Kerala developed an electronic ladies toilet near Kudesia Park in Kashmere Gate, which was to be a state-of-the-art facility. It did not occupy much space, got automatically locked, and would open for use when a coin of a particular denomination was inserted in the slot. The only glitch was that it used a lot of water. The toilet got installed near ISBT for demonstration; very few people, however, used

[12]DNA, 'Bio-toilet, electronic toilet: Delhi civic body's new experiments', accessed 19 June 2019, https://www.dnaindia.com/india/report-bio-toilet-electronic-toilet-delhi-civic-body-s-new-experiments-1423030

the toilet, as it was not free. The setting up of the three types of toilets could not be continued even at select places in the city due to paucity of time. The conventional toilets were therefore repaired and space was created on the walls in front of the toilets or urinals for commercial advertisements, with a view to involving the private sector through the PPP scheme. The arrangement was to allow private advertising companies to use the space free of cost and maintain the toilet facilities. The private companies got the agreement drafted in a manner that favoured them. However, soon they stopped maintaining the toilet facilities and the matter finally reached the courts. The sufferer was the common man, as the facilities could not be used due to poor maintenance. This is why all the public conveniences throughout the city have a characteristic stench. The requirement of setting up public conveniences throughout the city with a foolproof mechanism for their maintenance deserves priority. Most such facilities are seldom used due to poor maintenance, and therefore they need to be designed keeping in mind the volume of discharge.

GAMES VILLAGE: NO EASY GAME

The Commonwealth Games seemed to be thwarted due to a piece of news popularized by a section of the media in India and abroad that some officials of the Commonwealth Games Organising Committee, on their visit to New Delhi to check on the preparations, found the venue wanting in many ways and that they had expressed their unhappiness at the speed and quality of the work. I got a call from the then chief minister of Delhi, Sheila Dikshit, on 22 September. She wanted me to accompany her to the site of the Commonwealth Games Village near the Akshardham Temple. She took me around the village and asked me whether the MCD could get the unfinished tasks completed on a fast track. I assured the chief minister without blinking that we would do the needful within a week's time. I was confident that Team MCD was capable of undertaking any task and completing it, if guided, instructed and supported appropriately.

The tasks assigned included: the clearing of the accumulated kitchen wastes of the Commonwealth quarters that had piled up for days and weeks, the plugging of the holes in the temporary boundary wall around the village through which stray dogs by the dozens were sneaking into the premises of the village, cleaning up of the whole premises, controlling the menace of mosquitoes hovering over the premises thanks to the overflowing Yamuna, unclogging the sewer lines because the commodes in the washrooms when flushed did not clear the muck and also the removal of monkeys who came visiting. The tasks were simple and easy, but there was limited time and any delays could jeopardize the Games.

It was decided to deploy teams with sufficient manpower from the departments of the Corporation under the supervision of senior officers to oversee the execution of the work. The entry of personnel, tools and equipment into the Games Village was allowed under a prescribed protocol of security, and therefore, even the sandbags used to plug the holes in the temporary boundary walls of the complex were subjected to X-rays at the Millennium Park Bus Depot of Delhi Transport Corporation (DTC) before being allowed inside.

The workforce deployed inside the Games Village was served food packets by the authorities which were not fit for consumption. The food had gone stale, and naturally the karamcharis were in a state of rage and started protesting. It would have finished our efforts to redeem our pledge of finishing the preparations on time. I met the safai karamcharis and assured them that food from outside would be served to them. The workers were pacified and thereafter they worked wholeheartedly. It is to the credit of the workers and the employees of the MCD that all the tasks assigned were completed in time and to the satisfaction of all the stakeholders, even though the agency engaged by the DDA had expressed concern over the completion of the tasks, and dealing with the foul smell emanating from the drains near the Jawaharlal Nehru Stadium, where the Games were to be held, had everyone flummoxed.

The nallah flowing near the stadium carries the sewage from South Delhi areas into Yamuna River. The decaying sullage or waste water gets completely removed and carried to Yamuna River during the monsoon season. However, after the season, the force of whatever little quantity of water is being discharged from the households along with faecal matter is not sufficient to fully clear the muck, which remains stagnant throughout in the nallah and every day, with fresh additions, layers of decaying matter get deposited throughout.

The bad smell emanating from the nallah would envelop the stadium. When the then union home minister visited the stadium to supervise the preparations, he expressed concern about the foul smell and instructed the senior officers of the MHA to inform the commissioner of the MCD about the situation. I took the senior officers of the Corporation into the nallah to find if anything could be done, even if temporarily. There appeared no plausible solution to diffuse the bad smell. The obstruction in the free flow of the sullage was usually removed by fully clearing the 'cunnet'[13] in the drain. As the news of the problem spread, an agency came forward claiming it had a foolproof solution to completely remove the bad smell in about forty-eight hours by using a special strain of bacteria. The agency was told to demonstrate the claim first before further orders could be placed with it. The demonstration by the agency, however, was not found effective.

[13]Cunnet is a concrete channel constructed on the bottom surface of the drain

SEPARATING LANES FOR ROAD DISCIPLINE

Another major task was the regulation of traffic on the roads to be used for the transportation of players and of course the commuters.

A pilot project on the SP Mukherjee Marg, a road leading to the Old Delhi Railway Station from the Kauria Bridge and further, was chosen to create separate lanes for motorized vehicles, rickshaws and pedestrians. It is a road that connects, in a way, much of the other Delhi to Old Delhi. It took a few months to create separate lanes for the vehicles plying on it, to ensure the modal split in close coordination with the public authorities, including the Railways. This initiative particularly benefitted the commuters, who had to otherwise wait for hours to reach Chandni Chowk or the railway station from the Hanuman Mandir on the Ring Road near Nigambodh Ghat. The heavily congested front of the Old Delhi Railway Station got a perceptible relief. However, the movement on a few lanes had to be temporarily exercised by deploying security guards.

It is a veritable fact that after physical enforcement of the modal split, the travel time from Hanuman Mandir to the Town Hall reduced considerably. The security guards had to be withdrawn, and no sooner did that happen than the vehicles started moving all over the place, crossing from one lane to the other.

The owners of guest houses in Karol Bagh were also keen on experimenting with pedestrianization to demonstrate the positive impact of the absence of vehicles from the roads in busy market areas. A pilot project was taken up and concrete resting benches were erected on the side of the road. The project, however, could not progress, as some traders were opposed to the idea. The non-availability of enough parking slots in the area also came in the way of pedestrianization.

There were many lessons to be learnt from these efforts to redefine public spaces. It is possible to bring improvements and achieve targeted goals by adopting a balanced approach and by involving the stakeholders for the larger public good. The role of the officers heading the departments is important, as they are required to monitor the progress regularly and sort out any problem which may come in the way of the implementation of a scheme.

REGULARIZING VENDORS AND HAWKERS

The ubiquitous vendors and the mobile hawkers in the city sell affordable items, ranging from a variety of food, vegetables and ice creams to fast-moving consumer items and clothes in local neighbourhoods, making it convenient for the common man and the floating population to get their requirements without going to an established market further away. Most of the vendors squat outside shops for a fee paid to the shopkeepers, who have no right to charge a fee in the first place. The shopkeepers do not own the public spaces in front of their shops and they need to keep the areas free of encroachments. There is therefore a need to protect the hawkers from being fleeced by anyone, including the employees of the regulatory departments of the government or the local body.

It is necessary to encourage the creation of self-employment opportunities and regulate their activities in the larger public interest. Vendors need to be accommodated in vending zones and the hawkers should be allowed mobility in a specified area only. The vending zone should have all the infrastructural facilities with a proper layout plan and a robust system for the disposal of all kinds of wastes, on the lines of Dilli Haat near the INA market. The vending zones in each area should have functional and clean toilets to maintain proper hygiene. It may also be necessary to prescribe terms and conditions for the vendors and hawkers to weed out imposters and allot sites to only those who have Aadhaar Cards.

An attempt was made to assess the approximate number of genuine vendors and hawkers in the city in 2010–11 by conducting a photo survey of all the locations in the city. The agency given the task of conducting the survey discreetly, however, unwittingly gave it publicity, which in turn resulted in fake vendors and hawkers storming into the streets and other such public spaces. This defeated the main objective of the survey. The project had therefore to be abandoned even before it started. However, they still needed to be educated on good hygiene, as the disposal of the wastes, including ice cream wrappers, plastic plates and paper cups, is a serious concern.

A STATE-OF-THE-ART SLAUGHTERHOUSE

The slaughterhouse located at Idgah in the Paharganj zone had been operating for more than a hundred years before it was shifted to Ghazipur. The issue of closing down the Idgah slaughterhouse had been a hanging fire for almost two decades. The pollution from Idgah slaughterhouse (where not less than 12,000 animals were slaughtered daily, with another 20,000 waiting to be slaughtered in the foregrounds) was enormous and there were reports of the blood, offals and bones flowing into the Yamuna. The areas around the slaughterhouse, which had no arrangements to process the byproducts, were unfit for human habitation.

Going against its capacity of slaughtering 400 animals per day, around 10,000 to 12,000 animals (sheep, goats, buffaloes) were being slaughtered per day. For nearly two decades, in the absence of a notified area, the livestock market for sheep and goats was held on the road (a passage of about one acre), and so were the sections for buffaloes. About 200 livestock traders carried on their business of sale and purchase of 500–3,500 animals per day, which were brought from Rajasthan and Uttar Pradesh. Traders from Jammu and Kashmir, Noida, Gurgaon, Faridabad,

Ghaziabad, Ballabgarh and Sonepat purchased live animals from this market. Another 150 traders carried on the business of sale and purchase of buffaloes from the adjoining livestock market. The livestock traders had illegally constructed sixty-eight 'kharkas' (hutments) to keep their unsold animals inside the premises. There was no skin and hide godown inside the premises. The shopkeepers therefore sold the skin of slaughtered animals directly to the 200 skin traders, who carried away the skins and hides in rickshaws and three-wheelers to their private godowns in the nearby residential areas of Motia Khan and Qasab Pura. The blood from the skins trickled down on the roads during transportation, causing inconvenience to the general public and school-going children. The godowns, made of thatched roof, had portions open to the sky to release the fumes of the skins or hides, which polluted the surrounding areas enormously. There were no triparies (machines) for the cleaning of the intestines of the slaughtered animals, and therefore, the 250 gut cleaners cleaned them manually, causing insanitation and unhygienic conditions. The guts or intestines were transported to the factories to prepare suture material to be used after surgery.

A slaughterhouse should be provided with lairage facilities, i.e. enclosures where the animals are allowed to rest for twelve to twenty-four hours prior to their slaughtering, and where the doctors also perform ante-mortem examination of these animals. Since there were no such facilities at the Idgah slaughterhouse, the animals were slaughtered soon after purchasing them, with the doctors conducting a superficial ante-mortem examination. Further, the slaughtering of the animals took place under insanitary conditions, leading to contamination of the meat and other related items. The blood of the slaughtered animals was allowed to go to the sewer lines, as there were no effluent-treatment facilities. The old and outdated infrastructure or size of the sewer lines and drains was inadequate to bear the load of the liquid wastes, and therefore, the blood-stained water stagnated in the neighbourhood.

The High Court of Delhi issued directions to restrict the number of animals to be slaughtered per day to 2,500, as against the 8,000 to 12,000 animals being slaughtered daily till March 2004. The residents around the slaughterhouse were living in virtual hell, and there was no hope of any relief from anywhere. The butchers found the location in the heart of the city quite convenient and they were not bothered about the pollution as that was the responsibility of the Corporation, it being one of its obligatory functions laid down in the Municipal Act, 1957.

A modern slaughterhouse was constructed with an area of 10.5 acres at Ghazipur following the directions of the Supreme Court of India on 14 July 2004, which stated:

> The MCD shall construct a temporary slaughter house (Abattoir) in Ghazipur within six months from today. Thereafter immediately slaughtering

> activities as well as the trade in the cattle will be simultaneously shifted to Ghazipur. The concerned slaughterers and the traders in animals will be given suitable place to carry on their business even if it is on temporary basis. Simultaneously, MCD shall construct a modern slaughter house keeping in mind the future needs as directed by the previous court order. The MCD shall ensure that temporary slaughter house and shifting of the slaughter house situated presently at Idgah as well as trading in cattle is transferred to Ghazipur within six months from today. The modern slaughter house as directed by the Court also should be completed within two years from today in Ghazipur. The Central Government shall make available all the necessary funds (90 crores) as per estimation of MCD which includes the cost of a temporary abattoir at Ghazipur as also the modern abattoir at Ghazipur as directed in the earlier order of this Court.

The slaughterhouse at Ghazipur has lairage facilities; livestock markets for sheep, goats and buffaloes in an area of 4.5 acres and 3 acres respectively; sixty-eight kharkas in an area of 2 acres; a separate skin and hide godown; separate sections for Jhatka, Halal and buffaloes; an effluent treatment plant (ETP) of 1,750 KLD capacity; three triparies, one in each section for cleaning the goats and intestines of the animals; and a personal hygiene section for the butchers. Blood of the slaughtered animals is collected separately, from where it can be taken for any possible useful purpose—for instance, to prepare blood meal, which is a dry inert powder. It is one of the best-known synthetic sources of nitrogen and is used as an organic fertilizer and high-protein animal feed. It is also used in gardens to raise the nitrogen level of the soil.

There was total reluctance on the part of the butchers and other stakeholders to shift to the state-of-the-art slaughterhouse set up at Ghazipur. The authorities were in any case convinced about the desirability of shifting the slaughterhouse. They however did not want that any issue relating to this sensitive matter should get precipitated and embarrass the government.

There were however critical issues on the ground relating to the logistics and strategy of shifting the operations to the newly set up slaughterhouse. There are three sections in the slaughterhouse—the Jhatka, the Halal and the buffaloes section. It was decided to first shift the butchers of the Jhatka section, who were fewer in number, followed by the Halal section and finally the buffalo section. Arrangements were made for free transportation of butchers in hired DTC buses at 4.00 every morning. The Jhatka section started operating from Ghazipur. The butchers of the Halal section tried to pull some strings by bringing in political pressure, as their stakes were the highest. However, after giving sufficient time to them to brood over and reconcile to the ultimate reality, the operations in the Halal section were closed permanently and likewise the operation of the buffalo section was also closed permanently.

The slaughterhouse at Ghazipur is operating efficiently, as it has well-planned spaces, and that too in an air-conditioned environment. There is a well-designed animal market, where animals are kept as and when they come from other states like Rajasthan, Haryana, UP, Jammu and Kashmir, etc. The hygiene and the quality of the meat are certainly better now, and this is also appreciated by the stakeholders. Illegal slaughtering all over the city *does* take place even now. There is a need to stop such slaughtering in unauthorized places, as this is not only against the law of the land, but also pollutes the environment in and around such places. There is yet another area of concern which should be addressed at the earliest—no formal arrangements have been made so far for slaughtering of pigs.

A proposal was initiated sometime in 2010, just before the Commonwealth Games, on the ground that the food habits of the visitors from foreign countries do include meat of various kinds and pork was certainly one of the requirements. The proposal was not accepted at that time, since the provisions of the Master Plan 2021 did not allow the setting up of any slaughterhouse in the union territory of Delhi. Whereas no dispute could be raised with regard to such a provision in the Master Plan, it is certainly odd that no slaughterhouse would be allowed to be set up in Delhi. This only proves that several of the policy prescriptions of the Master Plan are devoid of ground-level requirements of the people. However, now the proposal has reportedly been considered for approval. The slaughter of pigs anywhere and anytime in open spaces could lead to severe problems, besides it being unhealthy. It is also a pity that pork is being sold without following the requisite safety norms needed to protect it from getting polluted or decayed and in the process creating health issues. The slaughter of pigs in the open poses environmental issues, as the intestines are quietly pushed into the drains or nallahs which finally travel down to Yamuna River.

PICK-AND-DROP FACILITY FOR STRAYS

There were many other initiatives taken by the MCD that deserve a mention. The stray dogs gathered around the Commonwealth Games Village could not enter the village complex to partake the leftovers being thrown from the kitchen in the area meant for collection of the garbage after the holes in the boundary walls were plugged. The dogs roaming along the boundary walls were defiling the surroundings of the Games Village. It was therefore considered necessary to shift the dogs away from the site. A building was identified for the purpose in Ghazipur area where they were kept for about twenty-five days, i.e. till the completion of the Games and then released at the same sites from where they were picked up. There were newspaper reports stating that the dogs had been whisked away to some areas in Greater Noida, which was not true. A langoor (baboon) was hired to chase away the monkeys from the Games Village. All the stadia were also required to be spruced up, and MCD teams of the various departments were deployed under the supervision of senior officers to do the needful.

SURPRISE INSPECTIONS

The periodical inspections, with a view to ascertaining the status and progress of the various schemes and programmes of the regular works of the local body, serve a useful purpose as they provide first-hand knowledge of the work being done on the ground. They also instil a sense of confidence and involvement in the official rung down the line. As it happens, prior intimation of the inspection does not give a true picture of the state of seriousness of the officers or officials concerned in the particular department. Further inspection of the projects while moving in a vehicle, due to the assumed paucity of time leaves wide gaps. The inspections need to be taken seriously, as otherwise the entire machinery down the line considers it business as usual, with no one to critically evaluate the performance. The 'surprise element' in inspections reveals the true picture of the way the work is progressing on the ground.

I remember a senior officer had confirmed the completion of some particular work assigned to him in a meeting. When informed that all the officers would visit the site after the meeting, the officer concerned developed cold feet and confessed that he had lied about the project work being completed.

The visits to schools, hospitals, etc. are important and this I realized quite early during my tenure in the Corporation. All the hospitals run by the local body had a remarkable makeover after regular inspections. The head of one of the hospitals was in the habit of inviting me quite often to visit the premises on one excuse or another, and I never disappointed him. He would however not take me for a round of the wards in the hospital and eventually when I visited the wards, I discovered the appalling state of affairs—the toilets had not been cleaned for months, to the extent that most of them were unusable and the medical superintendent could only fumble for words when asked for an explanation. The policies and programmes of the government and local bodies need to be implemented on the ground for which it is important to closely monitor the progress on a regular basis, as otherwise they remain on paper and there is a huge loss to the exchequer.

With Rajnath Singh, Defence Minister of India

Launching the MCD website in July 2008

Ravi Shankar Prasad, MP and then Member, Committee of Privileges of Parliament addressing a workshop on the DMC Act, 1957 and Master Plan 2021 in November 2009

Delivering the budget speech in the Standing Committee in 2009

MCD was presented the e-India Award in 2009 for its lead role in implementing e-Governance initiatives

Speaking at the inauguration of Dr Shyama Prasad Mukherjee Civic Centre in 2010. Also seen are the then Home Minister, P. Chidambaram, Former Deputy Prime Minister, L.K. Advani, Leader of the Opposition in the Lok Sabha, Sushma Swaraj, then Chief Minister of Delhi, Sheila Dikshit and then Finance Minister of Delhi, Dr A.K. Walia

Inauguration of private-public partnership (PPP) scheme in 2010, in the presence of Sushma Swaraj, then Leader of Opposition, Lok Sabha

Kushak and Sunahri Nallah Bus Parking and Prem Nagar Underpass being inaugurated by then Chief Minister of Delhi Sheila Dikshit in 2010

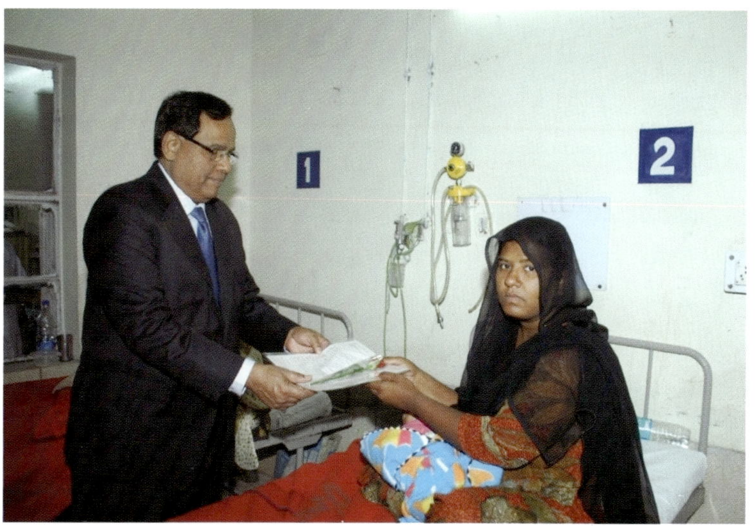

Handing over birth certificate of a newborn to its mother at the Kasturba Gandhi Hospital in 2011 after inaugurating the services

Welcoming Kapil Sibal, the then union minister for Human Resource Development

Receiving a cheque from the income tax department for leasing out space in the Civic Centre

Welcoming the Lt. Governor, Delhi, Tejendra Khanna

Greeting children in a decorated jeep at Dr Ambedkar Stadium on the occasion of Children's Day with Sushma Swaraj, the then Leader of the Opposition in the Lok Sabha and Mayor, Rajni Abbi

Handing over terminal benefits and memorabilia to a sanitation worker on the day of his retirement

Flagging off the mosquito terminator train that goes around railway tracks in Delhi equipped with power sprayers to kill mosquitoes and other insects

Addressing a gathering on the occasion of Gandhi Jayanti

FIVE

IMPLEMENTING THE REFORMS AGENDA

The Corporation has implemented significant reforms for the city with a view to augmenting revenue collection, improving service delivery and cutting down wasteful expenditure. The unified MCD witnessed the introduction of some of the best practices relating to the management of finances, revenue, expenditure and debt. Thousands of offices of the MCD spread throughout Delhi were provided with computers and connected through a 35 Mbps line using the modern multiprotocol label switching (MPLS) protocol. All the activities of the Corporation were re-engineered and automatized to bring in transparency and efficiency. In addition to its new avatar, the Corporation was also housed in new and swanky offices in the tallest building in Delhi—the Civic Centre.

FROM OLD TOWN HALL TO A SWANKY CIVIC CENTRE

The first impression of a government or a municipal office perhaps brings to mind images of a dilapidated building with worn-out furniture lying in total disarray, a few officials idling on their chairs, and work inevitably in a pending state. However, the shifting of office from the Town Hall to the newly constructed building of Civic Centre has given a new facelift to the offices of the MCD. I still remember the comment of a senior bureaucrat who had come visiting my office in the Civic Centre. The official said that he could easily compare the office with the offices of any of the corporates. The tallest, iconic and stately building of the Civic Centre is 112 metres high with twenty-eight storeys. The signature design of the building and its imposing structure are simply ineffable. The shifting was formally inaugurated by the then union minister of home affairs, P. Chidambaram, on 22 April 2010 and it was named Dr Shyama Prasad Mukherjee Civic Centre.[14] I have nostalgic memories of the days spent in the grand and magnificent Town Hall in Chandni Chowk, whose historical significance

[14]'MCD's Civic Centre building inaugurated', Zee News, 22 April 2010, accessed 19 June 2019, https://zeenews.india.com/news/delhi/mcds-civic-centre-building-inaugurated_621139.html

as the site of civic governance would remain fresh in public memory for all times to come. The meeting halls of the Town Hall are beautiful and have been witness to the deliberations of civic governance by elected representatives for almost half a century.

The Civic Centre, on the other hand, is an intelligently built building, fully air-conditioned with full power backup. The working desks or workstations of the officials are independent, giving them a feeling of ownership. The design of the Civic Centre building allows natural light to flow into the rooms. The underground parking space with two storeys accommodates all the vehicles of the officials, the councillors as well as the visitors. There is space for construction of at least two helipads on the roof from where one can have a panoramic view of the entire old city of Delhi, Lutyens Delhi and as far as the TV Tower in Pitampura and the Lotus Temple in Kalkaji. The auditorium in the Civic Centre has a seating capacity of almost 1,000.

There is a system for reusing the waste water, and also for reducing the consumption of power by the air-conditioners. Sensor lights which switch off or dim as the occupancy in a room thins out have been installed. The meeting halls in the Centre are equipped with state-of-the-art facilities and electronic gadgets, to effectively facilitate deliberations.

The efficiency of the officials improved substantially in the soothing environment of the Civic Centre. The seat of civic governance is well poised to function as the nerve centre (that was the original plan which was stymied by the trifurcation of the Corporation) and also for regulating, controlling and guiding all activities by putting them online and making the services directly accessible to the citizens.

DIGITAL INITIATIVES

The Corporation became the first public authority in the country to manage all transactions pertaining to outdoor advertisement through an online system. Also, by following a strategy of minimizing leakages by introducing the concept of damage charges on illegal displays by bringing more organizations under the umbrella of an advertisement revenue net, it was possible to enhance the revenue from advertisement tax by 64 per cent during the financial year 2010–11. Starting with the initiation of the biometric system for marking attendance of the regular as well as substitute employees, to going online for tax payment, to easing pressure on provision of civic services, transparency and transformation were achieved in every sphere of working of the MCD.

The introduction of the biometric system of attendance marking across all departments as well as all categories of staff brought discipline and punctuality, thereby improving the work output as well. The system was integrated with the payroll system to eliminate the chances of its disuse at a later stage.

MCD goes online: The e-Tendering application system has passed the test of time. Same is the case with the online submission of property tax and factory licensing. The health information system (HIS) has been of enormous use to better hospital administration and patient care. The MCD is the first organization in India to have made the right to information (RTI) application online. Even the building plan approval scheme developed by the Corporation is one of a kind in the entire country, which not only makes applying and tracking online possible, but even processing is computerized. The complex rules of business have been captured in the Building Plan software and are successfully tested for live situations. An application filed online generates an instantaneous acknowledgement, and after a while of processing, the system generates a statement for the citizens so that they can correct or complete the application in all respects.

It was proposed to switch over from an entirely manual environment to an e-environment with a view to breaking the general veil of opaqueness in providing the various services to the general public. The e-files were proposed to be introduced in place of physical files, which would ensure that no paperwork coming to the MCD would get lost or misplaced, nor would any paperwork be delayed, as the pendency of any file beyond a reasonable period of time would be captured by the system. The initiative to introduce transparency helped to identify the non-implementation of duplicate projects on paper.

PROJECTS ON PAPER

There were several projects being executed on paper only. Usually, in the rush of the financial year closing, there is a clamour to utilize the allocated funds lest it should lapse, irrespective of whether the project is useful or not. Projects implemented during the preceding years are put up for approval or evaluation by clumsily changing their titles and making them look like a new project in the hope that the scrutiny may only be superficial. There was a classical case—a project related to the relaying of a road from point A to point B. The project proposal aroused suspicion; inquiries were made by linking the proposal to the records of projects executed in the previous year. It was found that the project had already been approved.

Similarly, the culture of changing the railings used as road dividers every year had taken deep roots. The railings were removed from one stretch of the road and shifted elsewhere after painting them properly to give a new and fresh look.

The e-Governance system keeps track of each paper received in the MCD. The e-Governance project is used for preventive vigilance making the entire working of the Corporation—both internal and external (citizen centric)—transparent, thereby reducing the instances of corrupt practices and providing for quick, transparent service to the citizens as well as employees within the MCD. There is a dedicated Data Centre and an exclusive wide area network (WAN) for the Corporation. The WAN covers all departments of the MCD, including schools, hospitals, dispensaries, etc. The project has seventy-one modules to cover all internal and citizen-centric work of the MCD, which also helps to identify and take action to address project delays.

PROJECT DELAYS

It is not uncommon to see some projects being halted by stay orders issued by courts. I recall a stay order issued by a lower court staying demolition of a shop which was in the middle of the alignment of a flyover being constructed from Mayapuri Chowk and passing along Narayana. The volume of traffic on the Ring Road, particularly during peak hours, is very high, as it connects West Delhi to New Delhi and South Delhi. The building of this particular shop had severely constricted the passage, allowing just two buses to pass through in opposite directions. The narrow passage made thousands of vehicles (on either side) wait for hours. And this continued for months.

The stay order was challenged by the officers of the PWD of the Government of Delhi accompanied by full facts of the case, including the factors leading to public inconvenience and the wastage of fossil fuel. A prayer was made to vacate the stay to facilitate clearance of the blockage. The court appreciated the grounds adduced for getting the stay vacated. The widening of the passage by demolishing the structure not only provided more space for the vehicles to pass through, but it was also possible to complete the construction of the flyover, thereby doubling the space available to the vehicles on this stretch of the road. It is therefore necessary that such cases of blockades are taken up in right earnest in the respective fora for getting them removed expeditiously.

It has been my experience throughout that if a case is presented with all the facts in a coherent manner and the benefits to the general public are highlighted in an unambiguous way, the courts fully appreciate the genuine requirement, as they are also equally concerned for the public good.

REPLACEMENT OF OLD MACHINERY

There is an interesting incident relating to the supply of a heavy garbage-clearing machinery for which the sole supplier was a public-sector company working under the Ministry of Defence. There was a debate about the sourcing of the machinery. The view of the majority was to invite bids to replace the equipment for making the operations more efficient and economical. An officer in the Department of Environment Management Services at the middle level was dragging his feet and not submitting the proposal. With time, a few machineries went out of order, which disrupted garbage-clearing services at these garbage-dumping sites. The effect started being felt on the ground with piles of garbage increasing every day. The timing of the disruption—just a few days before the Commonwealth Games 2010—was chosen so as to bring disrepute to the country. The strategy of the company was to get the supply of old machines with obsolete technology effected, as then there would obviously be no requirement to purchase new machines for many years. The workers of the Corporation would continue struggling to improve operations which would, however, never happen.

I had to go and meet the secretary to the Government of India in the Department of Defence Production (of the Ministry of Defence) and request him to intervene in getting the machines repaired so that the disruption in the services at the dumping sites could be prevented, especially during the Commonwealth Games.

The characters involved in the drama were certain that once the issue is raised in this manner and if the operations at the dumping sites implode, it would force everybody concerned to press the panic button and the game would be over. The old machines would continue to operate and the issue would be forgotten once the heat was mitigated to tolerable levels.

Their sinister design did not succeed that time around, as the Corporation was determined to replace the old and redundant machines with modern, efficient ones. In hindsight,

I am able to recall the way an officer was covering up the plight of the machines, the operations and the issue itself; he would always bring up other issues to divert attention.

RISE IN REVENUE

With a view to introducing best management practices, the MCD initiated a comprehensive reforms programme. Financial reforms and introduction of modern financial practices were the mainstay of this initiative, launched in 2010. The Corporation's internal revenue includes taxes, rents, fees, fines and user charges. A significant aspect of the Civic Centre relates to the generation of revenue. The total built-up area of the Civic Centre is around 12 lakh sq. feet and so much area was not required for the headquarter office. It was decided to lease out around 45 per cent of the area thus fetching a revenue of ₹1,800 crore. The total cost of construction of the Centre was around ₹600 crore. There was, therefore, a net saving of ₹1,200 crore. The surplus area has been given to the Income Tax Department of the Government of India on a perpetual lease for ninety-nine years.

Financial reforms proved to be very successful, as the MCD's financial parameters and performance improved substantially. Following the successful introduction of an Internal Audit System, the MCD's revenues went up consistently between 2008 and 2012, particularly in property tax, advertisement tax, toll tax and various remuneration projects. The ratio of outstanding debt to current revenue declined from 63.6 per cent in financial year 2008 to 50 per cent in financial year 2010, and by efficient debt management in financial year 2010–11, the ratio decreased to 42 per cent. In order to have an objective assessment by an outside agency about the success of reforms, the MCD approached Fitch Ratings agency for an independent evaluation. Due to the MCD's sustained efforts at monitoring, control and financial planning, the agency rated the MCD with a long-term grading of AA-(IND), which indicates a high credit rating. This rating validated the reform achievements. Financial planning also enabled simplified computation and online payment of property tax.

The Corporation's citizen-friendly Unit Area Method of taxation implemented by the MCD from April 2004 has simplified the method of calculation of property tax.[15] Tax payers could easily calculate the tax payable themselves, using the laid down parameters. This did away with subjectivity in the assessment of property tax. Online system of filing tax returns and payment through convenient payment gateway have further improved the system. The augmentation of tax revenue was done by (a) enhancing tax rates, (b) widening the tax base and (c) closely monitoring the enforcement and recovery proceedings.

---

[15]https://commoncause.in/publication_details.php?id=294, accessed 19 June 2019

Another major reform was by way of toll tax collection through outsourcing. This led to an increase in the revenue collection from ₹54 crore in 2002–03 at a cost of ₹8.5 crore (approx.) on 1,400 personnel of the Corporation engaged in collection of toll tax (in addition to logistic arranged for collection of toll tax) to ₹192 crore at a cost of ₹30 lakh (approx.) per annum on twenty-five personnel of the Corporation.

The rates of toll tax were revised for the financial year 2011–12. For three years, starting from 16 May 2011, the Toll Tax Contract was awarded for ₹936 crore with an annual realization of ₹312 crore. The revenue from toll tax increased from ₹192 crore to ₹312 crore per annum, i.e. by 62.5 per cent. These are a few examples to illustrate the methods by which the revenue for the Corporation was further augmented.

The Corporation successfully implemented contract appointment through softwares developed locally called e-Recruitment, which automatically filtered eligible applications, ranked eligible applications on the basis of predetermined parameters, took care of the complicated reservation system and completed the procedure within a short time. The system eliminated human error and subjectivity while remaining transparent throughout.

All the employees in the MCD are administered through an Employees Information System (EIS) to monitor recruitments, transfers, postings, leaves, promotions, disciplinary proceedings, pensions, etc. and each employee has a unique ID linked with his or her biometric. The Engineering Department Information System contains several modules such as constructions, maintenance, building plan, quality control, etc. A comprehensive e-Governance project on turnkey basis covering all aspects of the Corporation was implemented in 2010.

WASTE MANAGEMENT

The state of the capital compelled initiatives to be taken in waste management, which included setting up of compost plants and waste-to-energy plants. Compost plants were set up at Okhla (200 metric ton [MT]), Bhalswa (300 MT) and Narela (APMC) (100 MT), while waste-to-energy plants were also set up at Okhla (2,050 tonnes per day [TPD]) and Ghazipur (1,300 TPD).

The waste-to-energy plant set up in Okhla is India's first such facility, which is also registered with the United Nations Framework Convention on Climate Change (UNFCCC) for earning carbon credits. The processing in the plant, which was synchronized with the BSES Grid, started functioning on 23 December 2011. It has till 8 July 2019 consumed 4.82 million tonnes of MSW and generated 1,029 million units of electricity in about eight years of its operation.

Even today, the work of processing of MSW continues in the three waste-to-energy plants set up by the erstwhile unified MCD. The plants at Okhla and Ghazipur consume 2,000 metric ton (MT) and 1,300 MT of MSW and produce 20 MW and 12 MW of energy respectively. As per the Technical Evaluation report of IIT Delhi, the refuse-derived fuel (RDF) route of combustion being adopted in the Ghazipur plant is more reliable than mass incineration.[16] Further, it was found that the project had been set up on an area measuring 5.63 acres, even as the standard requirement is 1 acre per 100 tonnes of waste. The use of European technology for boiler and Flue Gas Treatment System (FGTS) makes it a world-class waste-to-energy plant. The Ghazipur plant will help in saving over 213 acres of land valued at ₹20 billion (over the project period) and mitigate 8.2 million tonnes of Green House Gas (GHG) emission over the next twenty-five years, thus reducing global warming equivalent to removing all the cars on Delhi roads for hundred days.

Other measures to manage waste included setting up an Integrated Waste Processing Landfill Facility at Narela Bawana (1,000–4,000 MT). The waste-to-energy plant at Narela Bawana, spread over 100 acres, completely consumes 2,000 MT of MSW and generates 24 MW of energy.[17]

The first C&D waste recycling plant was also set up at

---

[16]https://commoncause.in/publication_details.php?id=294, accessed 19 June 2019

[17]TNN, 'North mayor says Bawana waste plant to hike capacity', *The Times of India*, 7 September 2017, accessed 19 June 2019, https://timesofindia.indiatimes.com/city/delhi/north-mayor-says-bawana-waste-plant-to-hike-capacity/articleshow/60399558.cms

Burari (500 TPD)[18] behind Model Town in North Delhi by the unified MCD that started functioning on 13 July 2009. This C&D waste processing facility has helped to ease the pressure of the 5,000 tonnes of C&D waste that Delhi generates per day, by recycling it into construction-grade aggregates. The capacity has been increased to 2,000 TPD.

Without new sites for development of a new landfill, reclamation of the Ghazipur landfill (2,000 TPD) was initiated. The findings of a report commissioned by the MCD in 2010 on the reclamation of Ghazipur landfill suggested that in Delhi where land is scarce and a highly priced commodity, finding a new site for development of another landfill is not an easy task. The expenditure required for closure and post-closure maintenance of the exhausted site and development of a new site would be very high. The best alternative is Landfill Mining and Reclamation. This option not only recovers the economic potential of the resources lying in the landfill but also saves a huge sum of money that would be otherwise used for capping and post-closure maintenance of the exhausted landfill and development of a new landfill. The process of Landfill Reclamation and Mining would be the most effective alternative economically, socially as well as environmentally. The report estimates revenue from sale of plastics, glass, leather or rubber clothes, metals, stones and

[18]Damini Nath, 'India's first plant that recycles construction waste', *The Hindu*, 29 August 2014, accessed 19 June 2019, https://www.thehindu.com/news/cities/Delhi/indias-first-plant-that-recycles-construction-waste/article6362727.ece

soil at around ₹310 crore from the Ghazipur landfill. The MCD also introduced door-to-door collection of garbage and even the sweeping of major roads through mechanical sweepers. All these waste-management measures helped to make Delhi a cleaner city.

The MCD also became the first civic body in the country to earn carbon credit in the form of Carbon Emission Reductions (CERs) following the implementation of the Clean Development Mechanism (CDM) project in its Okhla Composting Plant.

REMOVAL OF ENCROACHMENTS

Another key area where extensive work was done was in clearing encroachments, even at the cost of negative publicity; for example, in the case of an area illegally occupied by tonga owners.

Anyone familiar with Old Delhi would vouchsafe the kind of insanitary conditions created for decades by the tonga owners in front of Lok Nayak Jai Prakash Narayan Hospital (earlier known as Irwin Hospital). These tonga owners tied the horses near the footpaths and parked the tongas in such a way that they nearly occupied the entire footpath and in many cases, almost half of the road—a main road leading from Rajghat to New Delhi. The heaps of haystacks and the faeces and urine of the horses created an intolerable stink. Commuters in cars, buses, scooters or cycles had to go through a brief spell of hell until they crossed the area. The cruelty to the horses was clearly visible. These horses had weak structures, mutilated bodies and drooping eyes, suggestive of chronic fatigue due to overwork. The owners used them day and night, probably more interested in earning fast money than treating the horses in a humane manner. The insanitary conditions and pollution in front of the hospitals—four hospitals are in close proximity—was affecting the recovery of the patients. Besides being an eyesore, the settlement of the tonga owners hampered free and efficient movement of traffic. The public space occupied by them was an encroachment. But as the encroachment related to their livelihood, no one in the past had thought of relocating them. There was however a need to spruce up the entire area to sanitize the space in front of the hospitals. The issue of their livelihood was a matter of concern, as any practice that had been tolerated for decades could not simply be terminated abruptly. A series of meetings were held with their representatives. They were initiated into discussing the imperatives and possible alternatives. Most of them refused to even consider any proposal to relocate. All of them spurned the proposal offering them vending thadas (licenses) in Shastri Park in East Delhi. The offer of vending thadas was an exception being made in their case, as the policy for allotment of hawking sites was under the consideration of the Delhi government and thousands of applications were already pending. The tonga owners thought nothing would happen to them, as they had occupied the space for decades. But, there was an urgent need to sanitize the encroached space and find a solution for the welfare of the tonga owners as well as the public. But they remained stubborn and implacable, refusing to take possession of the vending thadas and engage in a new trade.

The cruelty to horses, the insanitary conditions and the resultant traffic chaos were reasons enough for shifting them out from the area, which had to be done with the use of force, following due procedure of law. The local MLA was very sore about it and came to meet me a number of times, advocating their rehabilitation. However, it was not possible to rehabilitate them, as with changing times, the modes of transport had improved. Older modes of transport, including tongas and bullock carts, were destined to wane. The entire area looked cleaner and free of any kind of filth after the encroachments were legally removed from the roadsides. There were many stakeholders who thanked the officers of the MCD for taking this bold decision.

The case illustrates the menace being caused in the city at innumerable locations with no hope of relief from encroachments and misuse of public spaces. The encroachments all over the city on the public pathways or roads occupy almost three-fourth of the space in the colonies and about half of the space on the radial roads. Even in the new areas developed in the last ten to fifteen years, encroachments have started making inroads, thereby reducing the usable spaces considerably. The rules and regulations need to be enforced more vigorously to convert all areas into 'no-tolerance zones', though in a phased manner and with a time-bound approach. Only a strong and determined political will can make such implementation of the rules possible.

The MCD also successfully introduced and completed major schemes in different parts of the city for upgrade of infrastructure under the transport, education and medical sectors, and community services. Upgrading these sectors relates primarily to construction and maintenance of roads, building of rooms in schools, construction of new wards in hospitals and building of community halls. A woman's hostel at Rohini was also constructed to provide hassle-free stay to working women. The hostel remains fully occupied. The financial assistance to widows for marriage of their daughters was enhanced from ₹20,000 to ₹25,000.

STAFF TRAINING

There is no lack of administrative acumen or competence in any way and in fact, many of the local officers in the Corporation are brilliant in almost all respects.

Efforts were, however, made to create a matrix of officers who could be used together to make the delivery of civic services more efficient. The participation of officers of the Corporation in many of the training programmes organized by the government for the organized services is almost negligible. Therefore, a certain percentage of officers in all categories was facilitated to undergo training at various levels for one to two weeks to give them the necessary exposure to various concepts.

The training of the lower cadres was equally important. The clerks and others face a maze when they join the service in the Corporation and it takes many years for them to even understand the basics of housekeeping—an important function which is the backbone of delivery of services of various types. Field-level functionaries such as the safai karamcharis, malis, domestic breeding checkers, etc. also required training to not only improve their efficiency but also to maximize the benefits which may accrue from the jobs they perform. For example, the safai karamcharis should not spread dust while sweeping the roads or push the collected garbage day after day into the drains alongside these roads, which eventually blocks the drains leading to waterlogging during the rainy season.

The malis of the Corporation were also required to be familiar with the names of plants and trees and the impact of planting various types of trees on the environment, besides knowing the where and when of planting the herbs and shrubs. The idea was to mitigate the harmful effects of pollution by proper selection of species of trees or plants.

All the reforms introduced in the working of the Corporation would yield optimum results only when pursued with the same zeal on a regular basis. Any laxity would easily throw back the sloth in the employees, who would be too happy to cross over to the same old routine of business as usual. It would also be necessary to further find solutions to accelerate the process of delivery of civic services to the people of Delhi.

SIX

REDEFINING URBAN GOVERNANCE

My experience as the commissioner of the MCD was a learning experience in one of the largest laboratories of civic governance, with its own successes and setbacks. Although the relative availability of basic requirements such as water and electricity is better in the capital as compared to other parts of the country, urban governance leaves much to be desired. For instance, the mushrooming of slums and unauthorized colonies, the unsystematic numbering of houses, the haphazard growth and unauthorized constructions are also not amenable to cleanliness and waste management. The delivery of civic services suffers as it is too difficult to access these areas, particularly by vehicles carrying load. Disposal of garbage and sanitation are constant challenges. So, what we have today is a fragmented city, as other than the planned New Delhi, the city is in a state of disarray with predominantly unauthorized built-up areas which defy all conventional solutions.

The three local bodies—the MCD (now divided into three bodies, namely the North, the South and the East Municipal Corporations), the NDMC and the DCB—look after civic services in their respective areas, which are well demarcated. The MCD is the main local body, as it caters to 97 per cent of the total population residing in the capital city. Most problems of urban governance have arisen in these areas that lie under the MCD.

PLAN EXECUTION

Making good plans, policies, schemes and programmes is not enough. It is more important to execute the plans and ensure their sustainability by the foolproof plugging of all loopholes.

An example of plans remaining on paper and abandoned halfway is the concept of integrated freight complexes (IFC) in Delhi. After an incident of fire breaking out in the paper market in Chawri Bazar, it was decided to set up multiple IFCs to decongest the old city. The IFCs were meant to be integrated with wholesale markets and to act as centres to offload and pick up wholesale goods by road and rail from and to other states.

The DDA acquired land for the setting up of IFCs and even allotted 621 plots of the available 995. However, due to the absence of essential services, those who had constructed buildings for the godown never occupied them and hundreds of jhuggies (settlements) sprung up in front of their offices. Many of those who had shifted returned to the old city areas, as the environment in and around the complex was not secure, hygienic and conducive to business.

Similarly, the IFC at Narela—spread over an area of 397.8 hectare—houses wholesale traders such as chemical, sanitary and hardware, textile, iron and steel, facility for warehouses, district centres and commercial spaces, a railway freight terminal, an ISBT, bus depot or metro connectivity and an automobile showroom. However, applications for allotment of land filed by various trade associations had elicited no response from government agencies. The DDA has given a list of fifty-odd documents and clearances required to get the building plans sanctioned. The lack of basic civic infrastructure and security is another factor for the failure. The IFC in Narela was the first of the five planned in the city in the early '90s, but not a single market has shifted till date.

These huge gaps between planning and execution need to be plugged, as they promote a culture of defiance of the legal authorities. There is also a cost for delayed projects that the administration needs to bear. Policymakers therefore need to decide policies and schemes which are feasible, and the process of implementation should begin only after all the imponderables are finally and fully settled.

Administrative challenges relate to making available usable public convenience facilities, upscaling the level of sanitation throughout the city, making public spaces and particularly roads and footpaths encroachment free, effectively controlling parking and advertisement spaces to augment revenue collection and further improving the level of transparency in all public service delivery systems. There is always scope for improvement in the way we look at problems or situations and the strategies to deal with them. While the cooperation of citizens can go a long way in keeping the city clean and free from disease-causing germs and pollution, a high level of coordination and cooperation is necessary between the government departments.

COORDINATION

It is the responsibility of the city's administrators and planners to provide reasonable living areas with basic facilities. The development of the basic infrastructure has, however, not kept pace with the requirement. The agency responsible for providing the facilities could not appropriately anticipate the requirements or even fully implement whatever they may have been planning. Many of the plans could not be implemented for reasons ranging from inaction on the part of the officers concerned to the change in priorities or requirements on the ground. The result is a city in which built forms are difficult to comprehend, manoeuver and keep free of insanitary conditions.

The city has grown almost wildly after the 1970s and the growth continues unabated. Everybody laments the state of affairs and blames the MCD for almost all the ills besetting the city. The facts are however to the contrary. The local body certainly is responsible for providing many facilities and for regulating urban development after the DDA hands over the approved colonies to the MCD. Other agencies and departments are also equally responsible for providing related facilities. The functioning of all these departments needs to be coordinated for the effective delivery of services and facilities. The nature of challenges is complex, but there are workable solutions.

UNAUTHORIZED DEVELOPMENT

Unauthorized colonies and constructions have taken over the city, putting tremendous pressure on management of basic needs and provision of civic services. It is largely the areas under the jurisdiction of the MCD that are predominantly unauthorized and unplanned as a result of free-for-all development. It is estimated that nearly three-fourth of Delhi is unauthorized. These unauthorized and unplanned constructions have happened primarily due to the laxity of the DDA on two accounts. First, even after the acquisition of 53,000 hectares of land as per the demand of the DDA, physical possession could be taken of around 37,000 hectares only.[19] Second, the DDA; being the custodian of land and planning for housing, also failed to protect the acquired land and use it for the construction of houses.

Another reason for the city's unplanned growth is the huge influx of migrants from all parts of the country, which leads to random jhuggi jhopri clusters all over the city since the early 1960s. Loosely guarded public spaces were occupied with impunity even though no basic facilities were available. This leads to open defecation, urination, squatting, burning of wood, charcoal, etc. in these spaces and also the creation of slums. A slum is a compact area with a population of at least 300 or about seventy households of poorly built congested tenements. These settlements grow in an unhygienic environment, usually with inadequate infrastructure and lacking in proper sanitation and drinking water facilities. Studies reveal that settlers in such clusters pursue informal economic activities, making a significant contribution to the city's economy, and over a period have established an interdependent relationship with the formal commercial, industrial and manufacturing functions in the city. From domestic help and unskilled factory jobs to semi-skilled and manual work, they constitute cheap labour and are an essential requirement of city's daily life.

---

[19]According to the Land and Building Department, Government of Delhi

However, the living conditions of the slum dwellers squatting in the fringes of the main city and in habitations on the banks of the nallahs carrying sewage from all over the city to Yamuna River are violative of basic human rights. The drinking water available in these areas smells of decaying fish, thanks to the ill maintenance of the supply lines, which has leakages. The pathways or stretches are so narrow that at some places, it may be difficult for two people to walk together. The stretches are also full of polythenes and other combustible materials collected by the residents from roadsides and other localities to eke out a living by selling these. Such areas are most prone to incidents of fire and the possibility of any outside help arriving on time is remote, as no vehicles—not even the smallest ones, let alone the ambulances or fire brigades—can reach inside.

The broad policy adopted in Delhi is that no fresh encroachments shall be permitted on public land and past encroachments that had been in existence will not be removed without providing alternatives. However, as most of these migrants are unskilled construction workers, low-wage earners in small-scale industrial units, petty traders and community service personnel, they are not willing to shift from their more convenient central location within the city to outlying areas away from their places of employment. This is due to the distance involved in commute and thus the extra commuting expenses. This is a major challenge for the state government and the local bodies. There is a need to curb the horizontal spread of the city and to begin with the redevelopment of the slums.

The database created by Delhi State Spatial Data Infrastructure (DSSDI) through its Special Purpose Vehicle known as Geospatial Delhi Limited (GSDL) could be used for appropriate planning to improve the living conditions of residents in slum areas, among others. The objective is to develop Delhi as a smart city by integrating geospatial data from all city departments for co-ordinated analysis, planning governance and management of resources. The data relating to all the departments would be integrated on a single map to provide single-window service to citizens and businesses.

LAPs of the wards with the predominance of slums may be prepared with active participation of all the stakeholders. The need to take the stakeholders on board cannot be overemphasized, as redevelopment can take place only with their participation. There may be concerns or apprehensions or vested interests and disinclination to change. It would be prudent to make the stakeholders familiar with the concept and the benefits which would accrue from the development.

In addition to unauthorized constructions in unauthorized colonies, there are a substantial number of violations of development control norms and building byelaws, even in regularized colonies.

There are cases of excessive ground coverage, extension of buildings over public streets, violation of height restriction and the construction of unauthorized balconies in the DDA as well as cooperative societies.

Around 75 per cent of the constructions in the city are not as per the prescribed building byelaws, which have been flouted and rendered these constructions unsafe. The capital's geographical placement in the zone of earthquakes, floods and strong winds mandates safety of the built environment. The exercise of sealing and demolition is certainly not the solution. Reconstruction of unsafe buildings—i.e. those that will not be able to withstand an earthquake of a severe intensity—is necessary to keep lives safe. How can the administration do this?

The strategy to renew the built environment either by retrofitting or by constructing these buildings all over again needs to be finalized carefully. For doing this, owners of these unauthorized buildings may be required to ensure that the construction of their buildings conforms to the building byelaws within a prescribed period. This is being suggested as houses and buildings are assets built with resources of the land.

The unauthorized constructions did not take place overnight. These have been a regular phenomenon over time. The causes of violations are many, but the policy of the government, though formulated with good intention, is primarily responsible for such a state of affairs, as when one single authority (DDA) is declared the sole custodian and developer of land, and all urbanizable land in Delhi is acquired and placed at the disposal of the DDA for the purpose of planned development, it is bound to lead to such a situation.

The anguish and disquiet of the citizens is quite evident when one reads comments the likes of which appeared in an article in *The Pioneer* (24 September 2006):

> For decades, the corruption and incompetence of city administration in Delhi have created artificial shortages by pushing law-abiding citizens and enterprises into the breaches of law. The basic condition of survival entails a tremendous flow of bribes to every city municipal and urban authority. Indeed, the state and its agencies have been the biggest violators of law here, engaging in outright fraud, abuse of power and falsification of government records and documents to engineer the distortions that envelop the city.

Inaction on the part of the DDA has led to all kinds of unauthorized development to the extent that it is not possible to rescue affected persons and property in times of calamities such quakes and fire accidents, like the one which happened in Hauz Khas, a colony in South Delhi, in the wee hours of 24 August 2016.[20] It took fire-fighting tenders

[20]NDTV, 'Fire In Delhi's Hauz Khas Village, 1 Found Dead', 24 August 2016, accessed 23 June 2019, https://www.ndtv.com/delhi-news/fire-in-hauz-khas-village-one-found-dead-1449520

an hour to reach the accident spot—a fire in a building—as the tenders had to be driven slowly due to the area being full of parked cars. Two tenders had to come back to the starting point. The Delhi Fire Service, the Delhi Police and the South Delhi MCD had candidly admitted in 2014 in an affidavit filed in the Delhi High Court that fire tenders and emergency vehicles could not enter the congested area. The narrow lanes do not allow a fire engine to reverse or return for a refill. This is the situation almost all over in the city, particularly in Old Delhi, East Delhi and the unauthorized colonies on the outskirts of Delhi.

All the constructions have taken maximum space leaving very little room for the movement of vehicles. It is therefore difficult to access such areas in times of emergencies. With no drain, no street, no road, no water supply, no outlet for waste water, no sewerage connection, no proper system of numbering the properties and garbage lying in heaps, it is total chaos. In the absence of water supply, local hand pumps for drinking water come up. Many lives were lost due to gastroenteritis in 1988 and there was an outrage. Who is to blame?

Posing another danger to public safety are the structures that are built one above the other even as the earth on which these are built is loose and cannot sustain any weight and certainly not of a building of four to five storeys. Due to the pressure of water almost throughout the year, the areas around the flood plains of Delhi are in a state of liquefaction. This means that the soil is almost semi-solid and it cannot sustain or hold any weight.

Yet, construction of buildings has been done in the area without taking care of the stability of the structures so much so there is no proper foundation for the weight-bearing walls which are resting on sand. In case there is collection of water around the area, which when drained with force (which may happen due to sudden rise and fall in the level of the river), it would take away the bottom surface, thereby disbalancing it. This is exactly what happened in the case of a building in Lalita Colony in Laxmi Nagar. The owner of the building had built four to five storeys on a structure like this and rented out each floor to nearly sixty vendors selling ice cream in the area. Around sixty-two people lost their lives as they got buried under the debris when the building collapsed.

Can we allow such urban settlements to remain health hazards and life hazards? The issue is enormously complex and mere legal formulation is not a constructive way forward. No amount of law and corrective measures will work as long as there is political elite that remains impervious to and exempt from justice.

In the face of large-scale urbanization and unauthorized construction, the infrastructure for the management of civic amenities, such as garbage collection, has suffered in the areas under the control of the MCD. The supply of civic services is a challenging task, as built forms in most areas do not conform to any rules or byelaws and even logic! Cleanliness is the prime casualty with serious repercussions, i.e. pollution.

WASTE MANAGEMENT

The status of cleanliness in cities and towns affects the overall well-being of its residents, directly or indirectly. Delhi produces around 10,000 MT of waste every day.[21] Besides 10,000 MT of MSW, Delhi generates 850 million gallons per day (MGD) of sewage and 269 MT of e-waste daily. As per estimates made by the World Bank, the generation of wastes in Indian cities would increase by 243 per cent during 2012–25.[22]

In a nationwide survey by the Ministry of Urban Development (Government of India), the areas under the MCD, where 97 per cent of the city's 16.7 million population lives, fared miserably with a rank of 397 among 476 cities and municipalities in thirty-one states and union territories, each with a population of over 10 lakh people.[23]

---

[21]Ashok Kumar, 'More e-waste by 2017', *The Hindu*, 2 March 2016, accessed 23 June 2019, https://www.thehindu.com/news/cities/Delhi/more-ewaste-by-2017/article8302222.ece

[22]Satwik Mudgal, 'Garbage gets attention', Down to Earth, 8 July 2015, accessed 23 June 2019, https://www.downtoearth.org.in/coverage/waste/garbage-gets-attention-46046

[23]Moushumi Das Gupta, 'Delhi one of the dirtiest cities, ranks low on Swachh list', *Hindustan Times*, accessed 23 June 2019, https://www.hindustantimes.com/delhi-news/delhi-one-of-the-dirtiest-cities-ranks-low-

Delhi generates around 4,000 MT of C&D waste, i.e. about 40 per cent of the total municipal wastes every day.

There are many sites in Delhi such as in Seelampur and Shastri Park, where tonnes of discarded electronics are manually dismantled each day.[24] The waste is handled in the open ground and broken down manually to extract recyclable metals to be resold, thus leaving both the workers and the soil exposed to toxic materials such as lead, cadmium, mercury and also the acid fumes generated in the process. According to experts, prolonged exposure to these can cause nausea, irritability, headaches, and liver and kidney problems in the long run. There is no disposal system at these places and the waste is eventually dumped into Yamuna River. Discarded electronic items are processed illegally through unofficial channels, since the operators are not authorized to collect or dispose of e-waste. The e-waste comes from distant places, even from outside Delhi. As per a study conducted jointly by ASSOCHAM and NEC, India has become the fifth-biggest producer of e-waste in the world.[25] India generates around 18.5 lakh MT of e-waste

---

on-swachh-list/story-Mf6qMpB6fgGgDIInjTEIIM.html

[24]Jasjeev Gandhiok, 'E-waste poses heavy metal threat', *The Times of India*, 11 May 2016, accessed 23 June 2019, https://timesofindia.indiatimes.com/city/delhi/E-waste-poses-heavy-metal-threat/articleshow/52213412.cms

[25]Jaideep Shenoy, 'India among the top five countries in e-waste generation: ASSOCHAM-NEC study', 4 June 2018, accessed 23 June 2019, https://timesofindia.indiatimes.com/india/india-among-the-top-five-countries-in-e-waste-generation-assocham-nec-study/articleshow/64448208.cms

each year with Delhi (9,800 MT) second on the list after Mumbai (1.2 lakh MT) as the biggest contributor (10 per cent being recycled in the formal recycling sectors and the rest by the informal sectors). There are around 103 crore mobile phone users in the country, which contribute to the extent of 25 per cent to the e-waste generated in the country. Household electronics account for 75 per cent of all e-waste generated, as most people are unaware of whom to approach to discard the old mobile phones, computers, laptops and other electronics devices. The e-waste rules 2016 specify targets for collection and recycling of e-waste. The authorities should insist on implementing the extended producer responsibility (EPR). The e-waste continues to pollute water bodies, groundwater and soil in informal recycling hubs in the city.

There is an urgent requirement to plan the infrastructure in such a manner that the collection of wastes, its transportation and final disposal happens in an efficient manner, which is not the case today. Garbage is the bane of the creators and the regulators.

House owners in the city are not much concerned where the kitchen and other wastes are taken by the workers. In congested colonies, garbage bags are thrown outside the house where it may lie for days and in some cases, even for months before it gets accidently picked up by the safai karamcharis.

Even the dhobis, particularly in the middle-class

colonies, use charcoal for ironing. In the process, they not only pollute the air but also the ground.

The habit of throwing the juices and the leaves of paan onto the streets creates a sanitation nuisance. Hawkers and vendors are culprits too. They park themselves at critical junctions on the roadside to sell their wares, causing traffic jams. Most have no arrangement for collecting the used paper plates and cups (usually made of plastic), which lie in heaps with flies and mosquitoes hovering over them.

While the activity derails the smooth flow of traffic and adds to pollution, it also contributes to the litter. It may sometimes take several days before these heaps are collected in special drives of cleanliness, usually coinciding with religious and social functions. Flies laden with faecal and other disease-causing substances also land on the sweets, cut fruits and other food items lying exposed in the shops all over the city—an open invitation to diseases.

The floating population also adds to the garbage or litter woes of the municipal officers, as they use and throw the cups and packaging material they bring with them on the roads and streets in the absence of designated receptacles for storing such waste.

The decomposition of wastes which starts immediately in every nook and corner of the city makes it a breeding place for all kinds of disease-causing germs. Even the municipal safai karamcharis find it difficult to regularly collect the wastes from all over the city, as the haphazard built environment leaves very little space to reach such locations.

STRUGGLING WITH SANITATION

The only time there is a total clean-up of the wastes from all over is during rainy season, when the wastes and filth get washed off almost completely, except from the garbage-dumping sites.

The 2,000 dalaos, the receptacles of garbage in the city, are expected to achieve a zero level of garbage at one point (of time) in a cycle of twenty-four hours, which perhaps never happens with the constant increase in garbage being dumped.

The dumping of waste in the open also leads to emission of GHGs, bad odour and also the spreading of windblown litter. The leachate—a kind of toxic soup created by the mixing of dew or rainwater with the waste at the garbage-dumping sites—seeps into the ground and pollutes the groundwater. The dumping sites as they are being managed pollute not only the groundwater but also the soil and air. The unscientific management of wastes is responsible for 25 per cent of the PM. Around twenty-two types of diseases can be prevented or controlled by improving MSW management.[26] There is an urgent need therefore to shift the receptacles under the ground

[26]'Solutions for solid waste management in India', accessed 23 June 2019, https://www.devalt.org/Pdf/L2_SixThemePdfs/trialogue2047 solid wastemgmt.pdf

at suitable locations all over the city. Customized containers of a sufficient capacity, say of 20 MT, could be kept under the ground and loaded onto the trucks using hydraulic system for transportation to the processing sites. Such an arrangement would help in storing the garbage in a concealed manner, thus preventing health or traffic hazards and nuisance to the general public. The space over the underground containers could be used for various purposes.

PUBLIC (IN)CONVENIENCES

An ineffective infrastructure for waste management impacts sanitation in the entire city, starting with public conveniences.

There are 3,000 public urinals and toilets in the city, that have become red spots for residents due to the unhygienic environment inside. The acrid and rancid smell around them would induce spontaneous vomiting and it is a pity that a strata of society with no other alternative uses such facilities by covering their mouths and nostrils.

The connections of these urinals or toilets to the sewer network usually remain blocked and with scarcely any water supply the situation hardly improves. In fact, it worsens during the monsoon when the entire faecal matter floats around in the toilets and even outside.

Around a million-odd vendors and hawkers all over the city use these facilities, and since there is no water to cleanse their limbs and hands, they carry the traces to the items they prepare and serve to millions. No wonder there are swelling crowds of patients in public hospitals and dispensaries for avoidable ailments.

There is large-scale open urination and defecation all around in the city, especially by slum-dwellers. As per the Delhi government data, there are hundred-odd slum clusters which do not have any toilet facilities. Colonies where public toilets have been provided are shunned by the people since they are hardly maintained. There are around 644 slum clusters in Delhi with only 473 functional toilets.[27] Result: Railway tracks serve as toilets for lakhs of people who reside in slum clusters. These tracks are the sites for open defecation, urination and garbage dumping, leading to ghastly sights and conditions. The safai karamcharis of the local bodies seldom go to the areas around the railway tracks, as they may disturb the users. Besides, it would not be appropriate to encroach upon the jurisdiction of the Railways. The conditions all around the railway tracks within the city limits are reprehensible, and there is a need to take steps to find a permanent solution to this issue. What is the solution then?

The railway tracks should be entrenched by boundary walls of an appropriate height on both sides up to the city limits, and the space on the surface of the boundary walls so created can be utilized for commercial use. The revenue thus generated could be used for the construction and maintenance of paid toilets of good quality along the

[27]As per the Delhi Urban Shelter Improvement Board (DUSIB)

boundary walls. The toilets should be connected to the sewer lines for ensuring effective discharge of the urine or faecal matter. The provision of a water connection to be kept functional throughout is a prerequisite.

Almost 50 per cent of the city is not connected to the sewer system and therefore, manual scavenging takes place even as Delhi banned scavenging in 2013.[28] The Employment of Manual Scavengers and Construction of Dry Latrines (Prohibition) Act, 1993 prohibits people from manually carrying human excreta and constructions or maintenance of dry latrines. Manual scavenging includes cleaning of drains and septic tanks and insanitary toilets that contain untreated sewage and human waste. Even in areas where a sewer network does exist, many do not take a sewer connection due to high cost.

Delhi has an extensive drainage system. It comprises of around 1,500 internal drains more than four-feet deep, which collect rainwater and waste water from residential areas and these fall into peripheral drains which join the main trunk drain and eventually, this whole mass of water gets discharged into the Yamuna. The length of natural drains in which the water flows with gravity is around 350 kilometres whereas the man-made drains, in which the water is required to be pumped up, cover a length of

---

[28]*Firstpost*, 'Delhi becomes first state to ban manual scavenging', 26 February 2013, accessed 23 June 2019, https://www.firstpost.com/india/delhi-becomes-first-state-to-ban-manual-scavenging-640831.html

around 1,700 kilometres.

However, the storm water drains or nallahs remain full of garbage to the brim as the safai karamcharis conveniently push the garbage into them, which, after mixing with moisture, become host sites for parasites and rodents.

The desilting of nallahs or the storm water drains takes place once in a year before the arrival of monsoon to prevent waterlogging in the city. Even then, waterlogging every season is the norm, as the nallahs carrying rainwater in many cases are fully settled and elsewhere, they are only half cleaned owing to the sheer lethargy of the nallah beldars engaged by the municipal corporation. The nallahs in the unauthorized colonies or regularized colonies do not have any connection to the drains for carrying the rainwater to Yamuna River and most of these areas become virtual ponds with the garbage floating all over, which in turn provides a safe breeding ground for mosquitoes causing malaria, dengue and other such diseases.

A study by IIT Delhi revealed that improper drainage system and the lack of a comprehensive mechanism for desilting tops the list of reasons for traffic jams in the city. The study revealed that several roads across the capital do not have properly designed slopes to help drain out rainwater. This is why a brief spell of rain is enough to bring the city's traffic to a standstill. Excessive and unchecked waterlogging not only adds to the jams but over a period of time, it also wears down the surface of the road.

ROAD MAINTENANCE

City roads have fallen victim to unauthorized parking and encroachments. Vehicle repair shops, roadside dhabas and vegetable and fruit stands hardly leave any space for the vehicles and even for pedestrians to move freely. In addition, poor drainage has rendered maintenance of roads an onerous task. However, Delhi already has more street space per capita than any other Indian city and laying of more roads is not the solution.

The main reason for the poor maintenance of roads in Delhi is lack of an adequate drainage system leading to formation of potholes every monsoon, which causes damage to vehicles and wastage of fossil fuel. There are a few vulnerable points which cause waterlogging every monsoon season. These need to be fixed because the losses thus accrued every year are considerable. The safai karamcharis of the local bodies, too, need to be instructed to not push any garbage or plastic into the bell mouths of the drains on the roads, as the free flow of storm water during the rainy season is thus obstructed.

Another cause for the poor quality of roads is the ill maintenance of public utilities. Any damage anywhere needs to be repaired on priority to prevent disruption of service, which is not possible without the digging of roads. Road maintenance authorities allow digging of roads subject to the condition that the dug-up roads would be restored to their original position. This however seldom happens. In most cases, the repair work is patchy and therefore the dug-up portion caves in when it rains.

The requirement therefore is to enforce a policy whereby the public utility is allowed to dig up the road and complete the work in a specified period. Also, in case the public utility does not complete the work within the specified period, it should pay damages or penalty at a prescribed rate per day. The cost involved in filling up the dug-up portion should be paid to the road maintenance authority by the public utility before digging a road. The cost of repair of the dug-up portion would be calculated by a prescribed formula of the government in this regard.

Or better still, the responsibility of construction and maintenance of roads in the city should be clearly laid down, for which it would be necessary to narrow down this jurisdiction to one single authority to avoid the usual blame game.

There is a classic example of a time when the entire country was watching the efforts of various authorities in Delhi to complete projects ahead of the Commonwealth Games 2010. The construction work in front of the Indira Gandhi Indoor Stadium, to build an additional road parallel to the Ring Road to join at the old iron bridge over the Yamuna, was being hastened to meet the deadline. The agency appointed by the PWD was working sincerely to win the race, unmindful of what its workers were doing. The Delhi Gate drain discharges much of the storm water from

Old Delhi into Yamuna River. The flyover being constructed passed over the drain. Debris, stones and materials were dropped quite heavily into this drain and one day when it rained heavily, the entire area was flooded with two feet of water.

The lesson from this incident is that a singular authority would have known the implications of any such accident and made suitable arrangements to prevent waterlogging on the National Highway No 1, close to Rajghat. One authority should therefore be held responsible and made answerable for the lapses in the maintenance of the roads.

Another cause for the traffic mayhem in the city is bad road design, such as the width of a road that suddenly narrows down, causing constriction of traffic or encroachments. On many roads in the capital, the right of way is occupied substantially by encroachments of all kinds and illegally parked cars. It is estimated that with the removal of roadside encroachments, movement of traffic would be faster and accident free, thereby bringing savings in terms of time as well as money.

PARKING CRISIS

The number of vehicles in Delhi surged 1.09 crore by March 2018 (according to the Economic Survey of Delhi 2018–19). More vehicles would be added year after year. One can find vehicles randomly parked on roads and footpaths, creating problems for pedestrians and vehicle owners. There is no quick solution.

A realistic solution is better public transport and stringent measures to control the use of personal vehicles. Experts point out that the increasing congestion in the capital roads is partly from buses ceding road space to private cars. Car owners pay a paltry sum as night parking charges during the registration of vehicles and virtually acquire the right to park on any public space. The manufacturers make a profit from selling cars where there is no cost involved in storing them. Parks have also been occupied for parking cars. There is a massive subsidy being provided to buyers. As per the Master Plan Delhi 2021, a car may occupy about 23 sq. mtr (about 250 sq. feet) of land when parked at its home base. This would include the actual parking space and a part of the driveway space. A similar amount of space would be occupied at its destination, such as the office. So the car effectively occupies about 46 sq. metres or about 500 sq. feet of space to be useful. The cost of this space works out to ₹2.76 crore (assuming the cost of land is ₹6 lakh per sq. metre in South Delhi). This space is provided either free or at a nominal charge of ₹20 for eight hours of parking. The parking charges should therefore be appropriately fixed by increasing the amount due after every two hours of parking and the rates of parking should be commensurate with the land prices of the area. There should be differentiated parking charges based on the congestion, land price, etc.

The parking facilities in the city need to be augmented by incorporating suitable and appropriate amendments in the relevant rules and acts. The citizens should not be allowed to park their personal vehicles on the road. Instead, they should create parking space at their home base and if that is not possible, they should be discouraged from purchasing vehicles. Authorities should ensure that no vehicles are parked in public spaces and if there is no alternative, vehicle owners should pay for doing so.

HIGH-RISE CITY PLANNING

The appalling state of uncleanliness of the city of Delhi, even including the posh areas has been aptly described by architect Gautam Bhatia.[29] He writes that:

> Delhi's unmanaged ah-hoc growth has effectively obliterated all notions of space and planning. At one point, the heart of the city was Connaught Place; a few decades later, the spread of district centres started to attract the population. Industries were then shifted to the outskirts. A few decades on, residential areas engulfed the same factory and industrial spaces which they were trying to escape. This uncontrolled expansion defeated a planned

[29]Gautam Bhatia, 'An ecological cul-de-sac for the Capital', *Hindustan Times*, 24 August 2015, accessed 30 May 2019, http://www.spaenvis.nic.in/arcindexx.aspx?langid=1&slid=1978&mid=2&sublinkid=1205

> separation. Today facilities like power plants, airports, army cantonment and highways which were intended for the outskirts have been absorbed in the sprawling expanse. In fact, the rationale for civic conditions is thwarted daily. People commute incessantly as their place for work and recreation are entirely unlinked to their homes. Meanwhile a cancerous river snakes it way through the centre of the town as much as the city's unmanaged waste is lying out in the streets or is choking its drains.

The capital's built environment needs to be systematically changed to reduce the demand on natural resources. The availability of land in the union territory for construction of houses stands almost exhausted. There is no scope of development for larger public good, as there is no space left for setting up schools, hospitals, dispensaries, recreation centres, community halls, etc. It would therefore be appropriate to shift focus on consolidation, rebuilding or retrofitting, creating common spaces, and converting slums and unauthorized colonies into liveable areas by involving the local population ward wise. The residents of a ward/ wards may be involved in planning by constituting groups of experts and builders.

Studies indicate that dense and high-rise cities provide more open space and consume less energy than those that are spread out, as there is less loss in the transmission of power and water. Energy savings are a plus. For instance, other dense cities around the world such as London, Paris, Berlin, Vienna, Singapore, Tokyo, Hong Kong, etc. consume below 20,000 million joules per capita, while sparser cities such as Houston and Phoenix consume nearly 80,000 million joules per capita. Higher floor area ratio (FAR) and densities give a range of environmental benefits and reduce the pressure on land, public transport and services.

Local areas too need to be redesigned for 'smart growth', in coordination with public transport infrastructure development and different levels of government. 'Smart Growth' practices create a more accessible city, control urban sprawl, support public transit, and make walking and cycling attractive.

An urban structure with a network of distinct, overlapping communities within which people can access on foot—within 800 metres or a ten-minute easy walk—most of the facilities and services should be the basis of planning. Besides saving time and energy, compact cities can have significant implication in saving fossil fuel consumption, climate change and environment. In Delhi, such a polycentric structure with new centres should be created along the metro and public transport corridors. The availability of play areas for children, schools, dispensaries, community centres, shopping areas, etc. would help in motivating stakeholders to become active partners in the process of reconstruction.

Redevelopment and reconstruction of the unauthorized and

weak structures may be taken up in a phased manner, which may take almost thirty years. A beginning however, needs to be made to provide safe and secure built environment and to facilitate sanitation and the availability of all services within a walking distance which would not only be environment friendly but there would also be substantial reduction in the requirement of power and water (by recycling used water for purposes other than for drinking).

RECORD OF RIGHTS

The city's municipal body is required to keep records of property ownership transfers in order to fix liability for payment of property tax. While revenue records, namely khasra, khatauni and jamabandi are being maintained by the Revenue Department for rural lands, there are no records maintained for urban properties.

A rural village may be declared as urbanized village under Section 507 of the Delhi Municipal Corporation Act, 1957, as a result provisions of Delhi Land Reforms Act cease to operate. There were 362 rural villages at the time of enactment of Delhi Land Reforms Act 1954 besides urban areas governed under Punjab Land Reforms Act and U.P. Land Revenue Laws. Nearly 135 villages have been declared as urbanized villages under Section 507 of the Delhi Municipal Corporation Act, 1957.

As most of the land in Delhi is owned by the Land

and Development Office (L&DO) and the DDA, they maintain complete records of the lessees in their property registers whenever a property changes hands on account of sale, inheritance, etc. The records are corrected to reflect the ownership status. After conversion of properties from leasehold to freehold, records are not being maintained.

It is a matter of serious concern that no records of rights are being maintained in respect of urban areas or colonies, namely colonies developed by developers like DLF, etc.; colonies developed by the Ministry of Rehabilitation and the DDA; unauthorized colonies which have not been regularized; unauthorized colonies which have been regularized after detailed layout plans approved by the MCD; Lal Dora where there is no record of rights in respect of individual abadi (populated) areas of urbanized villages.

There is a need therefore to create and maintain records of titles of immovable properties in urban areas which would reduce litigation, prevent encroachments and improve urban planning and tax collection. The provisions of the Delhi Survey Registration and record of Titles of Immovable Properties in Urban Areas Act 2009 therefore are required to be implemented in letter and spirit.

SOLUTIONS FOR A CLEAN CITY

The feeling that nothing can be done to make the city cleaner than what is being done by the municipal staff only reflects a kind of despondency. This needs to be shed from the mindset and appropriate solutions found to keep the city neat and clean and free from the risk factors causing epidemic-like situation year after year. The infrastructure for collection of wastes from the households, its transportation to the garbage-dumping sites and further processing of the waste's into useful products need to be tremendously improved by making investments. The investments are going to be huge; benefits of the investments however would be a kind of insurance against diseases. It would also make the citizens more productive. The garbage-dumping sites are already filled beyond their capacities. Delhi is a landlocked territory and there is no space available, nay being allowed by the local residents, as they do not want to have garbage piling up in their neighbourhoods. They all need a solution to the problem of garbage, yet do not allow the space to be used for this purpose. The successive dispensations, both at the Central and local levels, have been struggling for almost two decades or more to find or locate sites even at the behest of higher courts. There has however been no success so far and it is almost certain that there will not be any new site available for this purpose in the near future as well. Not to speak of a new site, the existing ones are also being sought to be closed by the local residents, for which demonstrations are held every now and then. This is a difficult pass. How does one reconcile to the harsh reality that even in the capital city it is not easy to find space for management of the garbage or waste? It is also a fact that in case effective steps are not taken immediately, management of garbage may emerge as an issue leading to a riotous situation all over the city. It is a kind of time bomb. If we do not bother to notice the writing on the wall, future generations will curse us for what we leave for them—a disease-ridden environment. A solution therefore needs to be found—a solution which is practical, useful and effective, irrespective of the costs involved, as there cannot be any talk of a trade-off in matters relating to sanitation.

SETTING UP OF THE DELHI SANITATION TASK FORCE (DSTF)

An agency known as the DSTF should be created as a limited company. The agency will be a separate entity with members in its governing body from the Government of India, Government of NCT of Delhi and the local bodies. It is considered necessary to hive off collection of garbage and all subsequent operations from the MCD to the DSTF—an autonomous Corporation to be formed on the lines of the Delhi Metro Rail Corporation (DMRC). This will insulate the DSTF from the ebbing efficiency of the bureaucracy of the MCD and create an efficient professional corps of sanitation staff who may be called the 'city keepers'. The DSTF shall be responsible for the collection of garbage from the households and its transportation to the processing sites; construction and maintenance of all drains other than those under the control of the Flood Control Department of Government of Delhi; management of sewage (a function to be transferred from the DJB to the agency); processing of all wastes, including C&D wastes; construction and maintenance of public conveniences throughout the city. The agency should also be authorized to collect annual sanitation charges from each household (excluding those below the poverty line) at the rate of ₹5,000, ₹4,000, ₹3,000, ₹2,000 and ₹1,000 of categories A, B, C, D and E respectively through the local bodies concerned. This would require amendment in the relevant rules or laws. The agency would also be responsible for the construction of the pits for the containers of a standard size or manufacturing the containers (for collection of garbage) of a very high quality to ensure durability. Minimum maintenance is of vital importance, as the success of the scheme is linked to the infrastructure for collecting and transporting the MSW to the processing sites. The work may be undertaken in a phased manner without disturbing the present arrangements, as it would take some time before the project becomes fully operational. The sweeping of roads should be undertaken between midnight and early morning—a task to be solely performed by the safai karamcharis of the local bodies. The norms for sweeping the roads need to be prescribed afresh keeping in mind that the road dust is one of the major contributors to pollution in the city. It would be the duty of the municipal safai karamcharis to separately collect the dust, sand or earth and not mix it with the MSW. The MSW collected from the roads would be deposited in the receptacles by the municipal staff and the sand or earth collected would be separately transported to the processing sites. The safai karamcharis should be advised suitably not to push the MSW, etc. into the drains. It is also considered necessary to audit the performance of the safai karamcharis of the local bodies through the Civil Society by appointing a committee for each area on a rotational basis. The name and designation of the sanitation staff need to be displayed on a board in each area. The audit team would report the performance of the sanitation staff online on a regular basis.

FROM WASTE TO ENERGY

The environment-compliant technology used in the waste-to-energy plant at Ghazipur would help in combating pollution in so far as it is caused by municipal wastes. Other plants should also adopt this technology and make them fully environment compliant. The processing plants are required to be operated at optimal capacity to utilize maximum quantity of garbage on a daily basis with a view to reducing pressure on the landfill sites. It would therefore be imperative to enhance the installed capacity of the existing plants while simultaneously planning for setting up new plants. The enhancement of installed capacity for handling more garbage and upgradation of technology would need investments. It may be worthwhile to examine whether there is any requirement of Viability Gap Funding (VGF) as per the established norms of the Government of India. Investment in processing of wastes would prevent spread of PM as well as around twenty-two diseases.

After entrenching the three garbage-dumping sites at Bhalswa, Ghazipur and Okhla, three more waste-to-energy plants should be set up at these sites. There is a need however to ensure that the emissions or effluents from the waste-to-energy plants are within permissible limits and the endeavour of the government should be to closely monitor the technology used in these plants.

Estimates indicate that around 85 per cent of the city's waste is collected from the streets and that over 50 per cent of Delhi's waste is fit for composting; 30 per cent is recyclable with just the remaining 20 per cent ideally fit for the landfills. It therefore would appear sensible to insist on segregation of the wastes at the household level, but that is easier said than done. It is also mandated by the waste management rules, but the ground reality is that even if the waste is segregated, it is collectively dumped at the sites, thereby serving no useful purpose. There is a need therefore to set up the facilities for segregation at the processing sites and also involve all the rag pickers in segregating the waste.

A pilot project recently initiated by an NGO with the assistance of rag pickers for facilitating segregation at the level of the households failed due to the reluctant attitude and in fact, hindrance from the residents. Another estimate suggests that around 3.5 lakh rag pickers alone recycle 25 per cent of the waste produced in the city and by default reduce GHG emission by approximately one million tonnes, that is equivalent to removing roughly 1,75,000 vehicles from Delhi's roads annually. It is true that rag pickers play a vital role in the management of wastes. Their services could be utilized at the processing sites for various activities, including segregation of the wastes. It is also necessary to help them guard against infection while in the process of segregating the wastes.

The collection of garbage from the households and its transportation to the landfill sites poses challenges which need to be met by creating mechanism and processes to ensure that the garbage remains concealed and not visible to the naked eye. All the dalaos where the MSW is collected should be converted into underground receptacles of garbage by using requisite technology. The collection of garbage from the households and its transportation to the processing sites should be done in two phases to make it efficient and economically viable. The first phase i.e. the primary phase should involve the collection of the garbage from the households to the underground receptacles located in each area within a distance of one kilometre. The secondary phase should involve the transportation of the containers (when they are full) to the designated processing sites. In the chain of collection of garbage, the primary phase should assume greater importance in view of the built forms in the city. The residents of each area should form Resident Welfare Associations to facilitate delivery of the garbage from the households to the team of the city keepers of the DSTF by making appropriate arrangements at their level. The garbage so collected would be deposited in the assigned underground container of the area without any slippages. The garbage would be received in a metallic container of 20–40 MT capacity embedded in the ground. The container would have two chambers: one for the MSW and the other below to receive the leachate from the MSW as it is squeezed to reduce the volume. The container when full would be loaded onto a truck with the help of a hydraulic machine (as used for washing cars) and the garbage shifted to the designated site for processing the wastes. As the filled container is taken out for clearance, an empty one will be put in its place to ensure that the smooth operation of garbage collection is not disrupted.

The container would be manned round the clock to ensure that not even a blade of grass is left on the ground. The container would only have an appropriately designed opening to receive the garbage and as it goes under the ground, the surface may be used as part of park, garden, road, etc.

It may be necessary for the Government of India to

issue suitable instructions to ensure that the acquisition of land and its allotment to the agency, the construction of the pits, and the acquisition of container or truck and all other required machineries are not delayed and that all the departments and undertakings extend full and unstinted support to the agency, as is being done for the DMRC. Even though garbage collection from within the city is streamlined, what is to be done with the garbage in the dumping areas remains the true test of urban governance.

The garbage-dumping sites at Bhalswa, Okhla and Ghazipur with ginormous piles of garbage are an eyesore, as thousands of tonnes of waste lying at these sites is decaying under anaerobic conditions generating landfill gases, which principally contains methane and carbon dioxide. Methane is a potential GHG, twenty-five times more potent than carbon dioxide in causing global warming. Therefore, the biggest challenge for the authorities all these years has been to find a solution to the ever-increasing mass of garbage lying at these sites. No new sites could be allotted by the DDA due to resistance from local residents. It is not likely that any sites for deposition of wastes would ever be allotted.

So, how can an increasing amount of garbage be managed within these three existing dumping sites in the future in a city with an ever-increasing population? Especially in the light of a study conducted by researchers in Italy that found people living within five kilometres of a landfill site are at an increased risk of developing lung cancer and respiratory diseases.

It is being considered that under the given circumstances, when no new site is available, the existing garbage-dumping sites are completely and effectively insulated from the outside world by constructing a wall of around 20 metres width and 120 metres height. It has been suggested that the C&D waste lying at the dumping sites could be used to construct the boundary walls in a phased manner. The findings of a test report of the samples taken from the dumping site at Ghazipur, found that the waste lying at the dumping sites has 63 per cent earth, aggregates, stone pillets and C&D waste; 7 per cent plastic and glass and the remaining 30 per cent organic waste which could be used for generation of electricity. According to an article in the *Hindustan Times* (25 August 2016), there is enough waste lying at the Ghazipur dumping site to construct the Delhi-Meerut Expressway—a 90-kilometre stretch on NH-24, approval for which is pending following a decision taken by the Council for Scientific and Industrial Research (CSIR) and Central Road Research Institute (CRRI) to support this project. The recycled waste will be mixed with bitumen among other processes to lay roads. The Railways, the PWD and such other road-constructing agencies should also be persuaded to utilize the inert waste for filling the potholes and road depressions.

In addition to a boundary wall around the garbage-dumping site, the ground-level surface of the site should be doubly insulated by using polythene of an appropriate width under RCC, also of an appropriate width, with a view to making it leachate proof for preventing its seepage into the ground. The entrance to the site should be designed so as to enshroud the activities inside the boundary wall. The connecting road to the site should be wide enough with at least four lanes on one side.

The huge space created by constructing the boundary walls with the C&D waste may be utilized for showcasing the prodigious inheritance of our antiquities, particularly the socio-cultural heritage of the country through murals and paintings. Some space may also be commercially exploited to earn revenue, which will help to recover the operational costs.

Simultaneously, the landfill sites must be made fully inert by extracting the trapped GHG. A beginning has been made at Ghazipur site by allowing the Gas Authority of India Limited (GAIL) to commercially exploit the trapped gases. GAIL is implementing a pilot project on a plot of four hectares in which the company would undertake to scientifically close the earmarked landfill site, and construct wells for extracting and flaring landfill gases, which would be enriched to natural gas quality for utilization as CNG. The residual inert garbage should be mandatorily lifted by bodies such as the Railways, the NHAI, the PWD, the DDA and other such agencies for filling up road depressions.

The steps for processing garbage should be clearly laid down under SOPs, which should include pre-processing with a view to segregating organically rich material, combustible materials and inerts. An Environment Management Plan should include initiatives for odour control, noise control and leachate treatment, besides social-inclusive programmes, such as the employment of rag pickers in the pre-processing plant. It would also be necessary to lay down emission norms for the waste-to-energy plants as well.

SEVEN

GO GREEN FOR A BETTER TOMORROW

The Master Plans of Delhi provided for the segregation of areas as per the nature of activities (residential, commercial, industrial), as well as an inviolable green belt, approximately one mile in depth, around the 1981 urbanized limits and urban villages on the periphery of the city. However, due to the exponential increase in the city's population and the resultant unplanned growth in the city, most of the goals, especially environmental, remained underachieved. The population of Delhi is estimated to touch 230 lakh by 2021,[30] which would further put pressure

[30]PTI, 'Delhi's population: 230 lakh by 2021', *The Times of India*, 14 March 2005, accessed 25 June 2019, https://timesofindia.indiatimes.com/city/delhi/Delhis-population-230-lakh-by-2021/articleshow/1051513.cms

on the ecology of the region, translating into increase in temperature and doubling of carbon dioxide emission.

Many factors, such as coal burning, industrial effluents, illegal fires and vehicular exhaust contribute to it, but the increasing pollution is also the result of rising population densities, and the proliferation of small-scale factories within the city limits and others that run illegally at night. Yet many of these illegal operations keep almost 40 per cent of the city's migrant labourers employed. Despite its density and zoning regulation, Delhi's sanitation and public health standards are abysmal, making the capital one of the most polluted cities in the world.[31] It is largely the scale and speed of urbanization that has put tremendous pressure on natural resources, such as water bodies, rivers, lakes, drains, ponds, groundwater, green areas, etc. which need to be cleaned and protected through the implementation of the law.

WHAT'S POLLUTING DELHI'S AIR?

Construction activities add huge amounts of noxious waste to Delhi's already polluted air. Globally, cities have employed legal processes to maximize reuse of such debris in construction. Singapore, which is a land-constrained country,

[31]Vijayta Lalwani, 'Delhi is one of the world's most polluted cities–So why is clean air not an election issue?' Scroll.in, 12 May 2019, accessed 23 June 2019, https://scroll.in/article/922922/delhi-is-one-of-the-worlds-most-polluted-cities-so-why-is-clean-air-not-an-election-issue

recycles 98 per cent of its C&D wastes (as of 2015).[32] In the UK, rules were amended in 2004 to allow the use of recycled aggregates. The C&D wastes include 2 per cent bitumen; 5 per cent metal; 23 per cent concrete; 31 per cent bricks and masonry; 36 per cent soil, sand and gravel. Construction dust causes respiratory disorders and damages lung tissues. As per a study published in the journal *Lancet Planetary Health*, air pollution from respirable PM 2.5 was responsible for 12.4 lakh deaths in India in 2017. The ultrafine PM (also known as PM I—one micron or less in diameter, i.e. two to five times tinier that PM 2.5 and thirty times smaller than the width of a single human hair) is the most dangerous among all PMs because it penetrates deep into the lungs and bloodstream. Other health hazards include lung dysfunction, asthma and headache, among others.

Air pollution is caused by vehicles, dust, roadside eateries, biomass, garbage burning, diesel generator sets, paints/varnish/adhesives, electric utilities, batteries, metal industry, coal, etc. Researchers from the University of Birmingham, IIT Delhi, CRRI and the Desert Research Institute (DRI) collaborated on a study on air pollution in India in 2013–14 and found that at a heavy traffic site on Mathura Road, an average of PM 2.5 concentration in winter was significantly higher than the standard. According

---

[32]Centre for Science and Development, 'CSE welcomes Delhi government decision on recycling of construction and demolition waste', accessed 25 June 2019, https://www.cseindia.org/cse-welcomes-delhi-government-decision-on-recycling-of-construction-and-demolition-waste-6007

to the report, several harmful components, including lead, zinc and polycyclic aromatic hydrocarbon were present in very high concentration in winter. The quantitative analysis done for the report shows that sources for the PM include soil, road dust and tail pipe emission from vehicles, wood, coal and waste burning.

Pollution is also blowing from other states into the NCR, i.e. from Haryana, UP and Rajasthan. The 900-acre Badarpur Thermal Power Station throws fly ash and contributes substantially to pollution as despite using water sprinklers and planting thousands of Ipomea plants, there is no way to stop fly ash from being airborne, especially during dust storms. There is at least 250 lakh MT of fly ash in the pond.[33] A report of IIT Kanpur flagged off fly ash as one of the major contributors to PM emission. According to the report, coal and fly ash contribute to around 37 per cent and 26 per cent of PM 10. The study also highlighted that the persistent presence of road dust and fly ash or coal particle encompasses Delhi like a layer. In summer, the atmosphere looks whitish to greyish, indicating the presence of a large amount of fly ash and dust. The fly ash however reduces significantly in winter when wind speed is low. A large amount of fly ash generation could also be from

---

[33]Richi Verma, 'Over 900 acres at Badarpur plant, ash flies in face of pollution', *The Times of India*, 10 May 2016, accessed 25 June 2019, https://timesofindia.indiatimes.com/city/delhi/Over-900-acres-at-Badarpur-plant-ash-flies-in-face-of-pollution-fight/articleshow/52196227.cms

batching plants (or concrete plants), which mix aggregates, cement and sand, for construction projects as the process uses pozzolan cement—a kind of cement having 35 per cent fly ash, which takes twenty-one days to settle, unlike Portland cement which settles quickly. Fly ash is sticky and toxic, unlike natural dust. It contains heavy metals, such as lead, chromium and aluminium. It also contains arsenic. It is bound to affect the airway causing allergies, increase the incidence of asthma, chronic obstructive pulmonary disorder and also the risk of cancer. The construction activities add a huge amount of noxious waste to Delhi's already polluted air.

Construction workers are also at risk of developing silicosis if they breathe high quantities of concrete and rock dust regularly. Demolition sites may release dust from asbestos, which is known to cause mesothelioma cancer and is banned in more than fifty countries.

BETTER CONSTRUCTION PRACTICES

There is an urgent need to adopt good construction practices, such as step-by-step demolition by covering the site during the demolition and sprinkling water to arrest the dust. Recycling of C&D waste can also contain the damage. The first C&D waste recycling plant set up at Burari behind Model Town in North Delhi by the unified MCD started functioning on 13 July 2009. The C&D waste is broken into small pieces in the recycling plant, to make aggregates used for laying of roads, paver blocks, etc. The impact has been positive. It has reduced the burden on the landfill sites which are already saturated beyond their capacities. There is a need to set up more such plants.

The C&D waste should be collected separately at designated sites throughout the city. The households or builders generating C&D waste would be mandated to deposit the waste at the designated sites after paying the prescribed fees to the DSTF. The household builders would notify to the DSTF in advance the registration number and type of vehicle engaged for transporting the C&D waste to the designated sites. It is quite likely that to avoid paying the requisite fees, the parties generating the waste may quietly deposit them on the roadsides during night time. The government should make rules and enact appropriate legislation to impose heavy fines or penalties on such lawbreakers to serve as a deterrent. A foolproof mechanism of locating the person illegally depositing the wastes may be finalized by the local body. The money collected as penalties would go to the local body to recover the cost of setting up the infrastructure for detecting such malpractices, etc others.

Large-scale urbanization leads to generation of more and more solid waste sewerage and effluents from various sources. The arrangements of processing the wastes for neutralizing the harmful effects are not sufficient to handle the full quantum of the wastes generated.

POLLUTION FROM STRAYS

Another source of pollution is the open garbage dumps that give stray animals, especially street dogs, unlimited access to feed on leftover food. They spread the garbage collected at places all over the city. It also adds to the pollution, as on being moved, the process of decomposition of the organic matter gets further hurtled. A clean city regulates the population of stray animals. Even if we got rid of dogs, they will be replaced by mice. Dogs are still easier to handle. There is a need, however, to control their population. The registration of pet dogs should be made mandatory with the installation of microchips to help identify owners in case of abandonment or loss. There should be a provision in the rules to penalize the owners if they abandon the dogs. The owners should be obligated to collect the faecal matter deposited by the dogs on the streets or roadsides and dispose it appropriately. The faeces of stray dogs should be removed by the sanitation staff of the local bodies too. According to a report that uses data from the World Society for the Protection of Animals (WSPA) and the Royal Society for the Protection of Cruelty to Animals (RSPCA), the best practice to control the population of stray is CNVR—collect, neuter, vaccinate and return to original place.

BIRD FEEDING NUISANCE

Another nuisance adding to the pollution woes of the city

is the feeding of birds on the streets, especially on traffic islands. Cars halt abruptly as people step out to feed the birds, mostly pigeons, which is a traffic hazard and adds to the mess. An article in the *Hindustan Times* stated that this oversupply of food and lack of natural predators has led to a population explosion of pigeons, a fast-breeding species.[34] The result is ominous—the common pigeons famously derided by Woody Allen as 'rats with wings' are everywhere. Pigeons are prolific poopers. Studies show pigeon droppings turn into concentrated salt unless properly cleaned. When dried droppings get wet, the compound can rust steel, thus slowly corroding structures. A pigeon dispenses about 25 pound (11.5 kg approx.) of excrement a year and bird droppings were estimated to cause approximately $1.1 billion damage in the US.[35] A number of foraging points in the city help pigeons grow in numbers. Pigeons are quick breeders, hatching chicks up to six times a year. Birds are adaptable, but they need to find food. The fact that humans are providing the pigeons food is disturbing the natural balance. People should realize that feeding pigeons does not guarantee themselves a spot in heaven but actually leaves them at risk of respiratory

[34]Shivani Singh, 'Why feed pigeons, dogs or monkeys in public places', *Hindustan Times*, 13 June 2016, accessed 25 June 2019, https://www.hindustantimes.com/columns/why-feed-pigeons-dogs-or-monkeys-in-public-places/story-XGbCyMBVsgZL4DECVSfuJN.html

[35]Dheeraj Jangra, 'Why you should not eat the pigeons', *The Times of India*, 13 October 2017, accessed 25 June 2019, https://toistudent.timesofindia.indiatimes.com/news/top-news/why-you-should-not-feed-the-pigeons/26235.html

disorders. Studies have found that fungi growing in dried bird droppings and feathers can lead to respiratory, pulmonary and skin diseases, which can sometimes be fatal. These birds are also carriers of fifty kinds of ectoparasites, including bed bugs and yellow mealworms that affect humans. About two-thirds of these pests may be detrimental to the general health and well-being of humans and domesticated animals.

Attics, cupolas, ledges, schools, offices, warehouses, mills, barns, parks, buildings and sign boards are typical roosting and nesting sites. The religious beliefs and practices are deep-rooted, but it is only by convincing the masses about the damage to health and the environment being caused by such a practice that it may be possible to reduce and eventually stop the practice of feeding birds.

MASTER PLAN FOR DRAINAGE

The management of sewage and storm water is another important area which needs to be effectively addressed for an unpolluted city. Almost 60 per cent of untreated sewage gets dumped into the Yamuna, thus translating into nearly 500 MGD.[36] There is a need to optimally utilize the installed capacity of the sewage treatment plants by simultaneously expanding the capacity to bridge the gap. This will help provide treatment facilities of sewage being generated in the

---

[36]http://sulabhenvis.nic.in/LatestNewsArchieve.aspx?Id=9722&Year=2016, accessed 23 June 2019

entire city. There are at present thirty-six treatment plants with a capacity of 640 MGD for sewage treatment. The capacity utilization however is low at 62.5 per cent with only around 390 MGD of sewage being treated, which means that around 460 MGD of sewage remains untreated.[37] Due to unauthorized constructions, there is no sewer system in 50 per cent area of Delhi. The sewage therefore gets mixed with waste water/rainwater and flows on to the roads. Yamuna traverses a distance of 48 km in Delhi. The 22-km stretch of the river from Wazirabad to Okhla receives about eighteen nallahs which discharge untreated sewage into the river. This is over and above the twenty-eight industrial estates which discharge almost untreated wastes which are full of harmful chemicals into the river. Medical waste from the hospitals and dispensaries also finds its way into the nallahs from where it reaches Yamuna River.

Thankfully, the Master Plan 2031 prepared by the DJB has a proposal/scheme to lay a 9,807-km-long sewer line with more than hundred pumping stations and around thirty-eight sewerage treatment plants at a cost of ₹10,077 crore.[38] The need therefore is to implement the Master Plan 2031 in a time-bound manner. The drainage system in Delhi comprises around 1,500 internal drains which collect rainwater and waste water from residential areas and these

[37]As per the Delhi Jal Board (DJB)

[38]Sushmita Sengupta, 'New Plan, Old Problem', Down to Earth, 17 August 2015, accessed 25 June 2019, https://www.downtoearth.org.in/coverage/new-plan-old-problem-47387

fall into peripheral drains which join the main trunk drain and eventually this whole mass of water gets discharged into the Yamuna. There are man-made drains which cover a length of 1,700 km and natural drains cover a length of 350 km. Whereas in the case of natural drains water flows with gravity, it is required to be pumped in the case of man-made drains. As a result of faulty designs of man-made drains, waterlogging in the city is a recurrent problem. Many drains have completely and fully settled.

A Master Plan for drainage is required, that could help facilitate discharge of water—both rainwater and waste water—into Yamuna River. This could save precious revenue of the government as at present, water is lifted mechanically and waterlogging severely damages roads which are required to be repaired year after year. The entire trans-Yamuna area is low lying and the rain or waste water needs to be lifted and pumped into the main trunk drain and discharged into Yamuna River on a daily basis by first collecting it in the sump wells. In case water is not regularly lifted and pumped, the entire East Delhi would get inundated. There is therefore a strong case for filling the depressions in East Delhi to bring the ground level in this entire part of Delhi above the level of trunk drains.

Scientific management of solid and liquid municipal wastes would yield benefits for the citizen in many ways. A study by the World Bank estimates that nearly 40 per cent of India's children are physically and cognitively stunted primarily because of lack of sanitation. A recent study by the UNICEF on the economic impact of sanitation has estimated that in an open defecation-free village each family saves over ₹50,000 per year on account of avoided medical costs, time savings and lives saved. There is a huge potential of generating wealth from waste through good solid and liquid resource management. It is therefore in the interest of all—individual citizens as well as the nation—to sustain scientific management of wastes. An average citizen considers waste management a waste of time, as somebody else will eventually clean up the surroundings. Nobody cares where the waste ends up, as long as it is not in their backyard. It is also known to everybody that waste is posing serious threats to our lives. All such citizens need to be properly and adequately informed about the harmful effects of insanitation in any form. Times are changing with the younger generations coming to terms with the reality. All citizens should join hands to keep their surroundings neat and clean at all times and make the city a better place to live, not only for themselves but also for posterity.

SAVING THE YAMUNA

It is a veritable truth that the Yamuna is being constricted and the floodplains have narrowed drastically between 1980 and 2014. According to a study published in 2014 in the *International Journal of Research in Engineering and*

Technology, the topographic and satellite maps indicate temporal variation in channel geometry and the position of the Yamuna. After 1980, the remaining floodplain areas were rapidly occupied by settlements, civic structures, roads, bridges, flyovers, playgrounds and metro stations. The flood plains of the Yamuna are the most important reservoirs for the city in times of crisis. The river is also being polluted heavily by the wastes or sewage being carried from all over Delhi by the eighteen-odd nallahs falling into the river. There is a tendency of dumping debris and wastes on the riverbed. The leftovers of havan are also thrown into the river. All efforts of the government to stop the citizens from throwing polythene bags, etc. into the river failed as the restrictive wire meshes intended to stop this were broken and stolen. The 200-km Hindon river originates from Purka Tanda village in UP's Saharanpur district. It meets the Yamuna near Delhi adding tonnes of sewage to the already choked river. Half-burnt human bodies are pushed into the river along with tonnes of ash, causing major bacterial pollution of the waters. Unless Delhi is clean, Yamuna can never be clean.

The residents of the unauthorized colonies use open drains to defecate and as the open drains are not connected to the sewage network, the faeces flow directly into the Yamuna. The river water is also being polluted by puja material and idols being immersed into the river as well as dairy wastes, soap and detergent, industrial wastes, etc. It is a sad fact that Delhi contributes 79 per cent of the total pollution load into Yamuna River even as the stretch of the river in Delhi is only 2 per cent of the total length of the river. Faecal matter is the major component of the pollution load in Delhi. The main reason for such a high percentage of excreta and untreated waste in the river is that around half of the population of the city lives in unauthorized colonies not covered by the sewage network. Most of the sewage from these colonies flows directly into the river. Some steps have been initiated to protect the river.

The setting up of an interceptor system to trap the sludge and other pollution material from these major drains—Najafgarh, Supplementary and Shahdara is a beginning in the right direction. It needs however to be assessed for its efficacy in ensuring that these drains do not pollute the Yamuna. The proposal of the DJB to treat the sewage by bio-remediation through activated wetlands and a series of floating wetlands needs to be pursued and implemented on priority. It is important to ensure that no kind of development takes place in the flood plains of the river. The squatters and jhuggi clusters are required to be removed from the river bank. The city drains should be fenced and regularly desilted. The general public and the safai karamcharis of the local bodies should be educated and appropriately guided not to dump garbage into the drains. It also needs to be ensured that no untreated discharge is pumped out in the UP and Haryana stretch of the river.

DELHI'S RIDGE AND WATER BODIES

There are very few cities anywhere in the world of the size of Delhi, which are fortunate enough to have a similar 'wilderness area' like the Ridge so close to the heart of the city. It is a major bird sanctuary and one of the oldest natural heritage sites in the world, besides being an invaluable source of fresh water for the surrounding areas. The survival of the living beings depends solely on the availability of water and the importance of the Ridge lies in the fact that it can provide pure mineral water for the whole city. Over the centuries, Yamuna River has shifted its course eastwards, leaving an alluvial plain and an extensive water cover in lakes, ponds and marshes. A survey by INTACH in 2001 revealed that there are at least 508 water bodies in the NCT of Delhi. However, the quality of water in these water bodies has deteriorated over the years and the building of embankments on the river has cut off their source. This has resulted in loss of aquatic and avian biodiversity, increased flooding and depleted water reserves under the pressure of urbanization. In the rural areas of Delhi, these bodies are being filled up and encroached upon to construct houses for extended families.

The cosmetic efforts of the sparring officers blaming each other for the loss cannot lead to restoration of these water bodies to their original status. The water bodies need to be looked after and all efforts to persuade citizens to harvest rainwater must be made with a scheme to provide funds from the government along with incentives. The mushrooming of the concrete jungle would require a customized design for harvesting the rainwater in view of the paucity of open, non-concrete spaces in the city.

It has been estimated that harvesting of the Yamuna in the last 200 years has polluted the water in the 22-km stretch along Delhi. The Yamuna flood plain can store 2 million cubic metres water in 100 sq. km (with an average depth of 40 metres) and can meet the requirements of six million residents in the city of Delhi.[39]

Therefore, development controls should be immediately placed on further building on the Yamuna bank, and its landscape should be zoned for productive and recreational uses. The recently constructed Yamuna Biodiversity Park, where more than seven acres of wet lands were created and also other kinds of aquatic landscapes that retain water and recharge the aquifers will be appropriate for this conservation zone.

INTACH's blueprint for water augmentation identified forty-four lakes and 355 village ponds as major sites for water storage and recharge locations. A few, such as Sanjay Lake are isolated water bodies while others like Najafgarh Jheel are connected with landscape through the Najafgarh drain. Restoration and connectedness of these urban wetlands and urban forest is imperative for the health of the ecosystems in the city. Delhi is defined by two natural

[39]As per the Delhi Development Authority (DDA)

features, Yamuna River and the Ridge, a part of the Aravalli Range of hills. Both of these carry essential water resources. So, all ancient and medieval cities were located either on the Ridge or on the banks of the Yamuna. The enduring value of such natural resources is being lost for short-term gain.

The Ridge forest, Delhi's oldest natural heritage, is sculpted on quartzite deposits, which have cracks from 2.5 billion years of natural history. The Ridge has valiantly borne the ravages of time but finds itself failing due to developmental activities in the last sixty years. All rain-fed aquifers surrounding the ridge are an incredible resource for pure water and must be preserved by protecting their recharge zones. The protection of the entire Ridge is crucial, as studies indicate that the only aquifers in Delhi that have good water are those recharged by the Ridge. Only a part of the Ridge area in Delhi is notified as reserve forest. A conservative 80 sq. km of Ridge forest area with a yet more conservative recharge potential of 50 per cent of rainfall and Delhi's average rainfall of 60 cm gives an annual recharge potential for the Ridge of over 20 million cubic meters (MCM).

The government has taken several steps to maintain the Ridge in its pristine form and to ensure that a boundary wall is constructed all around the vulnerable areas of the Ridge measuring around 7,784 hectares. The Ridge acts as an air purifier and an air-conditioner for the entire capital. Unfortunately, several areas, including Vasant Kunj, Jawaharlal Nehru University (JNU) and Rabindra Rangshala have come up on the Ridge before the government's 1996 notification which declared the Ridge Area a protected forest land.

Delhi suffers greatly from the urban heat island phenomenon—certain urban areas are extremely hot compared to others with less concretization or more green cover. A study by IIT Delhi found several parts of Delhi to be sizzling hot in summer. Areas like Connaught Place, Sita Ram Bazar and Bhikaji Cama Place had recorded a difference in temperature of about 8.3 degree celsius as compared to surrounding areas.[40] Urban forests can create the much-needed canopy cover.

The Ridge must be made into a valuable ecological asset for the city. At present, it is a degraded forest dominated by 'vilayati kikar', which edges out everything else to reign supreme.[41] The Ridge can be converted into an amazing rich dry forest and can also serve as a massive carbon sink.

The 80 hectare Tilpat Valley near Sainik Farm in South Delhi is important for its ability to retain water in many natural deep pits in the area. The catchment has degraded because of the shrinking forest cover. However, under the

---

[40]Times News Network, 'Plant a tree and clean the air', 4 August 2015, accessed 25 June 2019, http://epaperbeta.timesofindia.com/Article.aspx?eid=31808&articlexml=PLANT-A-TREE-AND-CLEAN-THE-AIR-04082015002008

[41]Mallica Joshi, 'How to uproot an ecology threat', *The Indian Express*, accessed 25 June 2019, https://indianexpress.com/article/explained/delhi-government-vilayati-kikar-removal-order-environmental-impact-5194797/

Biodiversity Project of the DDA in Tilpat Valley, one lakh saplings was to be planted and the valley was expected to start providing its ecological services to Delhi in about ten years when the canopy height of these saplings reach 25 to 30 feet. There are several benefits that this park will provide, such as improve the weather condition, ensure greater water recharge, act as a physical barrier to dust, prevent dry weather through transpiration, act as a carbon sink with the humus in the soil acting as a permanent store for carbon, absorb several pollutants and most importantly, act as a habitat for carnivores. The park has the potential to be a true wildlife habitat.

Delhi is one of the greenest cities in India with a 20 per cent forest cover.[42] It has nine city forests, which add to the forest cover of the city but are used to only provide space for compensatory afforestation. Fortunately, the fourteenth Finance Commission of India under the former RBI Governor re-enforced the idea of incentivizing states to retain their forest cover.[43] States have an additional responsibility towards management of the environment and climate change while creating conditions for sustainable growth and development.

However, plantation drives in the city, which are usually

---

[42]Mallica Joshi, 'Delhi one of the greenest cities, still falls way short of 33%', *Hindustan Times*, 5 August 2015

[43]Shreeshan Venkatesh, 'Fiscal branch', Down to Earth, 7 March 2016, accessed 25 June 2019, https://www.downtoearth.org.in/news/economy/fiscal-branch-52944

short-term initiatives with no care taken to ensure the survival of the planted saplings, mostly favour non-native varieties because of their appealing looks. But experts point out that trees native to an area adapt to its soil and ecology over hundreds of years. Such plants take care of themselves without draining resources such as groundwater. Exotics, on the other hand, are resource hungry and often crowd out native species. As the topographical soil in Delhi and the NCR varies widely, planting native trees suited to their requirement would facilitate their survival. For instance, species of Arjuna and Jamun around the Yamuna; Bahera in Delhi's roadside soil; Kardhai in the dry and rocky soil of the Ridge; Dhok in the porous dry Ridge soil as well as Neem that survives in hot weather with high density of SPM; Shesham which survives on the Yamuna bed; Indian Olibanum which is suited for dry rocky areas of the Ridge; Desi Ashok that adapts to hot weather and withstands waterlogging; Peepal, suited for Delhi's partly sandy and well-drained soil and Kachnar (also known as Bauhima) that thrives in sunny places.

The concept of city forests needs to be promoted and provided all assistance. By doing so, the onslaught of dust from outside the territorial limits of Delhi could be effectively contained and neutralized. Planting trees with broad leaves acts as a buffer zone around the city within a radius of half a kilometre width, which in turn would also act as a carbon sink and help to keep rising temperatures in check.

Meanwhile, the last and only virgin forest area of Delhi-NCR—Mangar Bani in the Faridabad district of Haryana—is under threat and urgently needs to be protected. The Bani is a block of forest area with dense tree cover that falls within Mangar and Bandhwari villages. The protected area measures 435 acres in Mangar and another 92 acres in Bandhwari. Mangar Bani is considered ecologically important by environmentalists and bird watchers.

Delhi's forest cover which was 26 sq. km in 1997 and 88 sq. km in 2000 (according to the Forest Survey of India) has attained around 200 sq. km coverage by now. It may also be beneficial to undertake afforestation of degraded forest lands, i.e. the Ridge area under the Urban Forestry Scheme of the Ministry of Environment and Forests.

There are around eighteen nallahs or natural storm water drains flowing across the city, which flow into Yamuna River at various points. The banks of these natural storm water drains have green cover consisting of herbs and shrubs and a sprinkling of Kikar trees which have come up on their own and provide shelter to birds, insects and reptiles. The banks of these natural storm water drains could be converted into protected forest areas through plantation drives and by selecting the right kind of species of trees which would strengthen the banks and also dissipate the bad smell in the adjoining residential areas.

There was a proposal in 2007–08 by the Government of Delhi to create a greenway over a length of 12.5 km of the Barapullah drain which would have ultimately been converted into a connecting road. But that would have thereby constricted the space for movement of storm water/sullage and also would have eaten into the green cover on the banks as has happened in some stretches on the bank of Najafgarh drain. These natural storm water drains should be allowed to remain as they are and the green cover increased further and the drains desilted regularly to allow for free movement of storm water or sullage.

I have heard stories of well-to-do families temporarily moving out of Delhi to escape the searing heat wave that singes the capital every summer. A long-term plan for mitigating the heat wave could be to plant trees along the periphery of the city.

It is important that we as citizens learn to live in close harmony with nature as any rakish exploitation of natural resources in whichever form would lead to intractable destruction of the environment. It is high time citizens, government and NGOs joined hands to stop all activities inimical to the ecology of the city.

EPILOGUE

Delhi is a city state, a microcosm of India. As villages evolved into townships and cities, there was a need to create a system of providing and regulating basic civic services. An organized system of providing basic services through a corporate body was first started in India in 1687 in Madras when Madras Municipal Corporation was formed. The seventy-fourth Constitutional amendment in 1992 provided constitutional status, mandating holding of elections in the local bodies every five years.

THE MANDATE FOR GOVERNANCE

The setting up of the Finance Commission for the distribution of taxes between the states and municipal bodies ensured flow of funds for the strengthening of the local bodies, which also encouraged them to generate their own revenues to sustain all obligatory as well as discretionary functions as provided in the twelfth Schedule of the Constitution. Obligatory functions such as sanitation, public health, regulation of places for the disposal of dead bodies, etc. fall solely in the jurisdiction of the local bodies and functions such as education, construction and maintenance of rest houses, etc. may be performed at their discretion subject to the availability of funds, among other factors.

Urban areas can be considered engines of economic growth and inclusion, and the city of Delhi has evolved into a metropolis which aspires to achieve global standards so far as infrastructural facilities and social services like sanitation, education and healthcare are concerned. However, the population of the city is growing at a rapid pace. It has increased about twenty-four-fold in the last six decades. The urban development in the city does not conform to any logic, perhaps due to the relaxed enforcement of regulations set up for construction of buildings. The infrastructure for civic services lags far behind the requirement causing inconvenience and hardships to the general public. The insanitary conditions all around in the city further add to the pollution in the city. The genesis of the unplanned urban development and the insanitary conditions needs to be properly understood to facilitate adoption of appropriate strategies. An initiative was taken by the erstwhile unified MCD to rebuild the unplanned areas to provide wide roads, space for common facilities and safe structures by involving the resident population. The LAPs prepared for thirty-three wards remain on the shelf due to jurisdictional issues and various other factors.

The constraints which act as impediments in the way of providing a clean environment need to be clearly identified with a futuristic perspective. This will facilitate the development of an approach with an inbuilt mechanism to deal with all foreseeable requirements in the distant future. There is an imperative need to think out of the box to find permanent solutions to the various ills besetting the city.

The issue of migration into the city in search of livelihood and better educational opportunities needs to be addressed appropriately and effectively. The NCR was planned to ease some of this pressure (both of migration and natural growth) off the NCT. The availability of multiple facilities in the city needs to be replicated in other areas of the NCR as well as in the adjoining states. This will reduce regular in-migration as well as a sizeable floating population that travels to the city to access medical care, education and other purposes for a short period of time.

The necessity of building an efficient and dependable network of medical care clinics with adequate infrastructure while also consolidating the existing network of primary healthcare facilities (both under the Government of Delhi and the local bodies) could hardly be overemphasized. The prevention of conditions and factors leading to diseases like malaria and dengue should be accorded high priority.

Delhi should aim towards becoming fully literate while ensuring that all residents have had basic schooling. It is also required to be ensured that there is 100 per cent transition of students till the secondary level of learning. To achieve this aim, it would be required to hire qualified teaching staff, employ optimum infrastructure and do regular assessment of students, teachers and educational institutions.

There are huge gaps with regard to provisioning of basic services and amenities between the poor and the non-poor localities. The need, therefore, is to equitably apportion availability of clean potable water, clean toilets, transport facilities—particularly feeder buses—and a minimum level of housing for the poor segment of society in a time-bound manner. The lack of sanitation, particularly in the areas inhabited by poorer sections of the population, is a challenge which needs to be addressed on priority.

Protection of the environment with a view to ensuring healthy living and a promising legacy for the future generations should occupy the centre stage. The non-availability of public toilets, open drains particularly in the slums, open garbage disposal and the resultant contamination of the surface water in the Yamuna are matters of serious concern. The uncontrolled flow of untreated wastes from human settlements as well as from industrial effluents and open defecation which ultimately travels down to Yamuna River via open drains have converted the river into a virtual nallah. Effective steps to stop contamination of the water in the Yamuna need to be further accentuated, as it is a lifeline of water availability for the capital city.

The maintenance of city roads is crucial for ensuring efficient movement of vehicles and for reducing pollution levels. Most of the roads need massive repairs after every monsoon season resulting in heavy recurrent losses to the exchequer. The arrangement for draining out storm and waste water leaves much to be desired. Poor drainage causes inconvenience to citizens and the resultant waterlogging leads to traffic jams. Stagnant pools of water are a breeding ground for mosquitoes causing malaria, dengue, etc. A Master Plan for drainage is imperative to make water flow with gravity. The entire trans-Yamuna area is low lying, and rain and waste water are required to be pumped into the main trunk drain and discharged into the Yamuna on a daily basis. The storm water drains in the old city area laid before Independence have fully settled. Sewer lines get punctured during monsoon and the entire muck flows onto the streets causing public health hazards. The Master Plan for drainage for Delhi has been prepared by IIT Delhi and it should make it possible for the authorities to address the recurring problem of waterlogging comprehensively.

The built environment of the city should conform to the provisions of the NBC 2005, the Master Plan and the building byelaws. The situation in Delhi is not at all satisfactory, as around 80 per cent of the structures are structurally unfit, which means that they may not be able to withstand an earthquake of a high magnitude. The growth of the built structures in the unplanned areas is such that there is hardly any space for the movement of vehicles to provide relief during emergencies. There is an urgent need to make all the structures safe. A policy of retrofitting on the basis of prioritization—i.e., buildings like schools, hospitals and key government offices would be given priority—needs to be formulated which should be implemented through a robust mechanism. Retrofitting is not an easy job, besides also being time consuming and expensive. Los Angeles took thirty years to retrofit its old buildings. A beginning should be made before it is too late!

All new constructions may be allowed water and electricity connections only after submission of a completion certificate from the local body. There are no proper records of ownership of properties thus leading to litigation and other related difficulties. There is a need, therefore, to create and maintain records of titles of immovable properties in urban areas which would reduce litigation, prevent encroachments and improve urban planning and tax collection. The provisions of the Delhi Survey Registration and records of titles of immovable properties in Urban Areas Act 2009 need to be implemented in letter and spirit.

The condition of sanitation in the city needs to be improved. The efforts of city planners and administrators for making Delhi a global city would remain an evanescent dream as long as insanitary conditions—in whatever form—

continue to exist. The superficial planning and execution of the various cleanliness schemes and projects will not take the mission of keeping Delhi clean anywhere. It is clear that by taking a broom and sweeping the roads advising people to segregate wastes is not yielding the desired results. There is the need for a paradigm shift in the approach towards waste management in a most comprehensive manner. We have been hearing about the multiplicity of authorities in the city as being the biggest stumbling block in the way of providing citizens a happy and healthy living. No efforts have however been made to reduce the number of authorities and agencies all these years. The numbers may have only increased. Therefore, now or never is the available time frame before the time bomb of insanitation explodes, bringing all activities to a grinding halt.

It is painful to note that precious time is being wasted in debates about the powers of the elected government in the city and the administrator of Delhi, known as the LG of Delhi. The constitutional provisions in this regard are crystal clear. Delhi is a union territory administered by the president of India through an administrator. Delhi cannot be equated with other states. The capital cities in federal countries around the world seem to have the same position. In several federal set-ups including the US, full statehood for the capital city has been demanded and rejected. Delhi was a state to begin with, from 1951 to 1956. The statehood was specifically taken away by the State Reorganisation

Commission which felt that the interests of Delhi's residents and its status as the seat of national government would be optimally balanced with Delhi being a union territory with a powerful municipal body. The Balakrishnan Committee whose 1989 report led to the present position of law recommended an elected legislative assembly but stopped well short of full statehood.

As rightly observed by the State Reorganisation Commission, there is a need to establish a powerful municipal body in the interest of Delhi's residents. However, in Delhi, just the opposite has happened with the trifurcation of the unified MCD on 2 May 2012. The unified Corporation was a strong municipal government of Delhi without any undue interference from the Government of Delhi.

The trifurcation of the unified MCD has shorn it of its powers, many of which stand transferred to the Government of Delhi. This has further put hurdles in the smooth functioning of the Corporation which suffered and still suffers late arrival of legitimate funds, thereby derailing all efforts made by the local body to provide efficient civic services to the citizens. It is, therefore, necessary to amalgamate the three Corporations—North, South and East—with a view to restoring the status quo-ante to constitute a unified MCD.

The MCD should be expressly given the mandate to make Delhi a truly global city in terms of cleanliness and other related infrastructural facilities. The flow of funds to the local body also needs to be ensured at the beginning of the financial year with a condition that the local body shall make all possible efforts to generate revenue from all possible sources, even from sources which have been hitherto left untouched due to whatever reason. There is a need to set targets and objectives at the beginning of the year with an annual appraisal at the end of the year by the LG of Delhi, who would submit a report to the Central Government about any requirements, deficiencies, etc. Let us strive to make Delhi a liveable city, worthy of emulation by other cities all around the world!

ACKNOWLEDGEMENTS

This book is based on my personal experience of the state of things in the capital city of Delhi. Hence, hundreds of people have contributed to it. I have also consulted newspaper articles, reportage of seminars, Master Plans of Delhi and Delhi Human Development reports, among others for this venture.

I am thankful to B.N. Singh, Mayank Sharma, A.J. Kurien, Deep Chand Mathur, Pradeep Khandelwal and Dr R.B.S. Tyagi—my erstwhile colleagues in the MCD—who spared time to go through the manuscript and provided their valuable suggestions.

I would be failing in my duty without thanking Nisha Sharma and Avinash Sharma, who typed the manuscript. And last but not least, my four-legged children, Gauri and Sheikhu, who helped me stay fit—physically and emotionally—to think and write.

I am grateful to Kapish Mehra, Managing Director, Rupa Publications and his team, comprising Yamini Chowdhury, Manali Das, Aasha Swarup and Sourya Majumder for their wholehearted support and enthusiasm.

INDEX